the
naked
cookbook

the
naked
cookbook

tess ward

photography by columbus leth

ten speed press
berkeley

introduction

Over the years the word "diet" as we understand it has changed. *The Naked Cookbook's* interpretation is based on the Latin origins of the word, *diata*, meaning "way of life." To me a diet is exactly that—not a quick fix, but a sustained way of eating that naturally supports our overall health and happiness.

Few people I know would claim that they follow their ideal diet, although this seems to be what everyone aspires to. Many of us still subscribe to the idea of "diet" in the short term, and its promise to change, help, or improve us. Lose the tummy, have slimmer thighs or a tighter butt, because it will make us happier, right? Why else diet other than to improve our quality of life in some way? So many of these unrealistic regimes claim to do this, and they may well succeed in the short term. But anything beyond the initial "starve yourself for a few weeks and lose weight" goes uncovered. In fact, any form of longevity is pretty much ignored, meaning dieters ultimately end up at the bottom of the heap, feeling worse than they did before they started. Too many diets are based too heavily in theory and not in practice. What works for one person is completely different for another. The area of nutrition and diet is full of contradictory information and evidence. There simply isn't a "perfect diet" or "one diet that fits all"; instead, it's about finding the best balance in one's own body.

The most important thing is to have a balanced understanding of what your own body truly needs. *The Naked Cookbook* moves away from processed and refined foods, unrealistic diets, and fad regimes; instead, it is about eating food in its most naked form.

A year ago, a restricted diet was something I was all too familiar with. Not for weight, but for health reasons. At age eighteen, I'd spent a month traveling in India. Along the way I picked up a parasite that I was to live with for the next five years. Over this period there were repeat visits to doctors and specialists. I was diagnosed with postinfectious irritable bowel syndrome, given more antibiotics than a dairy cow, and put on a restrictive diet. It wasn't until I met Humphrey Bacchus, a clinical nutritionist and medicine practitioner, that my problem was finally diagnosed.

The recipes in this book are a compilation of the foods I have uncovered and created on my journey back to full health. The recipes have been designed to support and fuel your body, encouraging optimal health through simple, delicious, and stripped-back recipes.

To clarify, this book is not strictly oriented toward any specific health-related diet. The recipes are naturally low in carbohydrates, free from processed food, and contain no refined sugar, but they are not gluten-free, dairy-free, or vegan (although many can be adapted to accommodate these diets).

This book is all about eating food in its purest form. *The Naked Cookbook* celebrates creativity in cooking, and all the recipes are efficient, practical, and packed full of taste. They have been inspired by all the wonderful chefs I have worked with and the countries, cuisines, and restaurants I have enjoyed. I hope you find my naked dishes as pleasurable to make, eat, and use as I have found discovering and creating them. Cook naked, eat happy, and you'll never have to do the dreaded "diet" again.

naked broths + stocks

Broths and stocks are typically made with bones and can include a small amount of meat adhering to the bones, which are often roasted first to improve flavor. Broths are simmered for a long period of time (often in excess of 24 hours), whereas stocks are simmered for 3 to 4 hours.

broth's goodness

Broth's long cooking time helps to extract as many minerals and nutrients as possible from the bones. At the end of cooking, the minerals have leached from the bones into the broth and the bones crumble when pressed between your thumb and index finger.

Broths are extraordinarily rich in nutrients—particularly minerals and amino acids, especially glycine, proline, and arginine. Glycine supports the body's detoxification process and is used in the synthesis of hemoglobin, bile salts, and other naturally occurring chemicals within the body, as well as supporting digestion and the secretion of gastric acids. Proline, especially when paired with vitamin C, supports good skin health. And there is evidence to suggest that arginine helps to improve the body's cardiovascular system.

Bone broths are also rich in gelatin, which improves collagen status, supporting skin health and also aiding digestive health.

stock's goodness

Stock is rich in both minerals and gelatin. Chicken stock, in particular, inhibits neutrophil (a type of white blood cell), migration; it helps ease the symptoms of colds, flu, and upper respiratory infections.

basic roast chicken stock/broth

1 leftover roast chicken carcass
2½ cups vegetable scraps
  (celery leaves, onion
  trimmings, leeks, fennel,
  carrot peelings, garlic, etc.)
2 bay leaves
A few thyme sprigs
Handful of parsley sprigs

1 Put the chicken carcass, vegetable scraps, and herbs into a stockpot.

2 Pour in enough cold water to cover the carcass by 2 inches, about 4 cups. Cover, bring to a boil, then decrease the heat to low and simmer, covered, for 3 hours (for stock) or for 24 hours or longer (for broth), occasionally skimming off any scum that rises to the top. If making broth, add water as needed to keep the carcass covered and cook until the bones become flexible and rubbery.

3 Strain through a fine-mesh strainer and pour into jars. The broth should gel, but it is not necessary. Store in the refrigerator for up to 3 days, or freeze for up to 1 month.

Asian chicken stock/broth:
Replace the vegetable scraps, bay leaves, thyme, and parsley with a 2-inch piece fresh ginger, 1 star anise, 3 or 4 fresh chile peppers, 1 whole garlic bulb (unpeeled and smashed), and a 4-inch stalk lemongrass (optional).

Makes about 3½ cups

beef stock/broth

Roasting the bones ensures a good flavor in the resulting beef stock. If making soup with this broth, it's wise to serve it very hot, as it may gel once it cools.

6 to 6½ pounds grass-fed
  beef bones
2½ cups vegetable scraps
  (celery leaves, onion
  trimmings, leeks, fennel,
  carrot peelings, garlic, etc.)
2 to 3 bay leaves
A few thyme sprigs
2 rosemary sprigs

1 Preheat the oven to 400°F. Rinse the bones, dry, and spread in a roasting pan (they should fit in a single layer).

2 Roast for about 1 hour, then remove from the oven and drain off any fat. Put the bones into a stockpot along with the vegetable scraps. Add cold water to cover, about 4 cups, cover, bring to a boil, and add the herbs. Decrease the heat and simmer, covered, for at least 3 hours (for stock) and up to 24 hours (for broth), occasionally skimming off any foam.

3 Strain through a fine-mesh strainer and pour into jars. The stock should set like gelatin and the fat should rise to the top. Remove the fat and set aside for cooking. To serve as soup, scoop out the gelled stock and reheat.

4 Store in the refrigerator for 2 to 3 days, or freeze for up to 1 month.

Makes about 3½ cups

fish stock

The best fish bones for stock are from fine fish—ask your fish supplier to remove the gills behind the cheek flaps to prevent any bitterness. Don't use the bones of oily fish. This is not as extravagant as it sounds, as fish suppliers will often hand over the bones for free.

1 pound, 2 ounces fish bones
1 carrot, finely diced
1 celery stalk, finely diced
1 onion, finely diced
12 parsley sprigs and 3 or
  4 fennel bulb trimmings
  (optional)
1 bay leaf

1 Put all the ingredients into a stockpot and add cold water to cover by about 1¼ inches. Cover, bring to a boil, and spoon off any white or gray froth that rises to the surface. Decrease the heat and simmer, covered, for 20 to 25 minutes.

2 Strain through a fine-mesh strainer into a bowl and let cool.

3 Store in the refrigerator for 2 to 3 days, or freeze for up to 1 month.

Makes 6 to 8 cups

miso soup

Miso soup is a traditional Japanese broth made from fermented soybeans. It is high in manganese, copper, and zinc and is a good source of protein and dietary fiber. As a fermented food, it is also beneficial to digestive health. The microorganisms used in the fermentation of soy miso can actively help metabolize proteins, carbohydrates, and fats, transforming them into smaller, more easily digested molecules.

1 tablespoon shredded nori or
  wakame seaweed (optional)
1 packet (¼ ounce) bonito fish
  stock, or dashi
2 to 3 tablespoons miso
  (any kind)
2 green onions, minced
½ block (7 ounces) firm silken
  tofu, cut into 1-inch cubes
  (optional)

1 Bring 4 cups water to a simmer in a pan and add the seaweed (if using). Simmer for 5 minutes, then decrease the heat to very low and add the remaining ingredients. Stir until the miso is well dissolved, then remove from the heat. Don't let the miso boil, as this will kill the beneficial nutrients and alter the soup's flavor. Serve hot.

Serves 4

naked infused oils

The quality of the oil you select depends on what you want to use it for. For instance, if you are making chile oil to use as a condiment, then use a high-quality extra-virgin. But if you are just intending to cook with it, then a more basic olive oil is more suitable.

It is important to use dried rather than fresh ingredients, such as herbs and chiles, to infuse your oil. Fresh spices and herbs release moisture that can cause bacteria to form in the oil (the only exception being garlic). If you are going to include ingredients with any potential moisture in your infusions, make sure you dry them out completely before using. It is also important to sterilize the jars before use (see the ghee recipe on page 17).

To make the infused oil last longer, you can heat it with the infusing ingredients, which kills any bacteria. To do this, combine the oil and other ingredients in a small saucepan and place over low heat for about 5 minutes, until the oil gets hot (but don't let it boil). Remove from the heat, cover, and let cool to room temperature. Transfer the other ingredients to a sterilized bottle, then add the oil and seal. It will keep for 2 to 3 months.

However, don't heat extra-virgin oil, as it damages the quality and the health benefits of the oil. Although this means this kind of infused oil won't keep as long (only around 2 to 3 weeks), you can just reduce the quantity that you make.

For these infused oils (pictured opposite), use a generous 2 cups of extra-virgin or regular olive oil.

chile oil
(pictured top left on opposite page)

10 to 20 small dried red chiles

garlic oil
(pictured bottom left on opposite page)

6 garlic cloves, peeled and halved

rosemary + bay oil
(pictured top right on opposite page)

2 large dried rosemary sprigs
4 bay leaves

lemon + pink peppercorn oil
(pictured bottom right on opposite page)

Zest of 2 lemons, cut into thin strips
2 tablespoons pink peppercorns

1 Leave the zest to dry in a warm place for 1 week before using. Or use the oil heating method.

naked dips

easy goat milk ricotta

(pictured top left on opposite page)

I have a bit of a bee in my bonnet about store-bought ricotta. Firstly, it is almost always rubbery, and secondly, there is seldom an organic option. Since it is so easy to make, I do it myself. I would recommend using a thermometer, but you can do it by eye—just watch the milk like a hawk!

Generous 2 cups whole goat (or buffalo) milk
¼ teaspoon fine sea salt
2 tablespoons freshly squeezed lemon juice

1 Line a colander with 4 layers of cheesecloth or 2 layers of food-safe paper towels and set the colander over a large bowl.

2 Put the milk, salt, and lemon juice in a saucepan and bring to a boil over a medium-low heat, stirring constantly. At this point the milk should begin to separate into solid white curds and translucent liquid whey. If only half of the milk is curdling, add a few more drops of lemon juice.

3 Using a slotted spoon, transfer the separated curds to the lined colander, cover it with plastic wrap, and let drain for a few minutes if you like it quite soft, or longer if you want it firmer.

4 Discard the liquid whey and store the ricotta in a sealed container in the refrigerator for up to 5 days.

Makes about 1 cup

wasabi crème fraîche

(pictured bottom right on opposite page)

A dollop of wasabi is all that is needed to add a mustardy kick to any dish.

6 heaping tablespoons crème fraîche
2 teaspoons wasabi paste

1 Mix the crème fraîche with the wasabi paste in a small bowl or jar. Cover and store in the refrigerator for a week or so.

Makes about ½ cup

---

coconut salsa

(pictured top right on opposite page + page 27)

This spicy salsa makes an ideal accompaniment to soups. For a dairy-free version, swap the Greek yogurt for coconut yogurt.

1⅔ cups unsweetened shredded dried coconut
1¾ cups plain Greek yogurt
3 tablespoons chopped cilantro
1 long green chile, seeded and minced
1 teaspoon freshly squeezed lime juice
½ teaspoon sea salt

1 Place the coconut in a bowl with 3 to 4 tablespoons hot water and let soften for 5 minutes. When water has absorbed, mix in the rest of the ingredients. Store salsa in a sealed container in the refrigerator for up to 5 days.

Makes about 2 cups

cucumber, radish + goat cheese raita

(pictured bottom left on opposite page)

The goat cheese adds a creamy richness to this raita, making it perfect as a condiment and dip, and also as a filling for wraps, like the gluten-free crepes (page 80). A little tip: Slice open the garlic and remove the germ (the little green piece inside the garlic); this will prevent the garlic from repeating on you when you eat it raw.

1 large cucumber, halved lengthwise and seeded
1¾ cups plain Greek yogurt
5 ounces soft goat cheese
1 large garlic clove, minced
Juice of ½ lemon
7 ounces firm radishes, very finely sliced
3 tablespoons chopped mint leaves
Fine sea salt and freshly ground black pepper

1 Slice each seeded cucumber half very finely.

2 Place the yogurt in a bowl and, using the back of a fork, mash in the goat cheese. Gently fold in the cucumber, garlic, lemon juice, half of the radishes, and the mint and season with a generous pinch of salt and pepper. Top with the remaining radishes and serve. Store the raita in a sealed container in the refrigerator for up to 5 days.

Makes about 2 cups

naked yogurts

basil yogurt dressing

1½ tablespoons plain
   yogurt with live cultures
¼ cup basil leaves, minced
¼ cup extra-virgin olive oil
2 tablespoons apple cider
   vinegar
2 teaspoons maple syrup
2 garlic cloves, mashed to
   a pulp
Sea salt and freshly ground
   black pepper

1 Mix all the ingredients together
in a small bowl, adding salt and
pepper to taste. Store in a sealed
container in the refrigerator for up
to 4 days.

Makes 1 cup

cumin yogurt dressing

3 tablespoons plain yogurt
   with live cultures
1 garlic clove, minced
1 tablespoon apple cider
   vinegar
½ teaspoon honey
2 tablespoons extra-virgin
   olive oil
1 teaspoon cumin seeds,
   toasted and crushed
Pinch of ground coriander
Sea salt and freshly ground
   black pepper

1 Mix all the ingredients together
in a small bowl, adding salt and
pepper to taste. Store in a sealed
container in the refrigerator for up
to 4 days.

Makes 1 cup

cilantro yogurt dressing

5 tablespoons plain
   Greek yogurt
2 tablespoons cilantro
   leaves, chopped
½ teaspoon cumin seeds,
   toasted and crushed
1 teaspoon maple syrup
1 teaspoon freshly squeezed
   lemon juice
1 garlic clove, minced
1 teaspoon extra-virgin olive oil
Sea salt and freshly ground
   black pepper

1 Mix all the ingredients together
in a small bowl, adding salt and
pepper to taste. Store in a sealed
container in the refrigerator for up
to 4 days.

Makes 1 cup

sauces

chunky peanut dipping sauce

3 tablespoons unsalted
   chunky peanut butter
2 teaspoons toasted
   sesame oil
2 tablespoons tamari
2 teaspoons apple cider
   vinegar
1 tablespoon honey
Juice of 1 orange

1 Put all the ingredients into
a jar and shake well.

2 Spoon into a bowl before
serving. Store in a sealed
container in the refrigerator
for up to 4 days.

Serves 2

Thai dipping sauce

1 tablespoon toasted
   sesame oil
2 tablespoons freshly
   squeezed lime juice
2 tablespoons fish sauce
1 fresh red chile, minced
1½ to 2 tablespoons honey

1 Whisk all the ingredients
together in a glass.

2 Spoon into a bowl before
serving. Store in a sealed
container in the refrigerator
for up to 4 days.

Serves 2 to 4

red cacao sauce

1 tablespoon coconut oil
½ teaspoon ground cumin
½ teaspoon spicy smoked
   paprika
1 onion, minced
Sea salt
2 garlic cloves, minced
1 (8-ounce) can diced tomatoes
8 cilantro sprigs, chopped
1 pitted date
1 tablespoon raw cacao
   powder
1 tablespoon smooth
   cashew butter
1 tablespoon freshly squeezed
   lime juice
Freshly ground black pepper

1 Melt the coconut oil in a skillet,
add the cumin and paprika, and
cook, stirring frequently, for a
couple of minutes. Add the onion
and 2 pinches of salt and sauté
until softened. Stir in the garlic
and cook for another couple
of minutes.

2 Stir in the tomatoes and cook
for 5 minutes, then transfer to a
blender. Add the cilantro, date,
cacao powder, cashew butter,
and lime juice and 2 tablespoons
of water. Blend on high speed,
adding more water as needed to
achieve the desired consistency.
Season with salt and pepper
to taste. Store in a sealed
container in the refrigerator
for up to 4 days.

Serves 2

naked dressings

Possibly more vital than the dish itself is the dressing. Whether you are pouring, dipping, or drizzling them or using them as a condiment, it is great to have a selection in your repertoire. I often keep a couple of jars of my different naked dressings in the refrigerator for speedy use. For all dressings (barring the ghee), put the ingredients into a small jar, put a lid on, and shake well to mix, then season to taste. Store dressings in a sealed jar in the refrigerator for up to a week.

tamari dressing

(pictured bottom right on opposite page)

3 tablespoons tamari
2 tablespoons apple cider
    vinegar
Finely grated zest and juice
    of 1 lime
1 tablespoon honey
½ garlic clove, minced
Pinch of finely grated fresh
    ginger
1 tablespoon toasted
    sesame oil

Makes about ½ cup

tahini dressing

(pictured middle left on opposite page)

2 tablespoons tahini
2 tablespoons tamari
2 tablespoons apple cider
    vinegar
Finely grated zest and juice
    of 1 orange
½ garlic clove, finely chopped
1 teaspoon finely grated
    fresh ginger
1 tablespoon toasted
    sesame oil
Freshly ground black pepper
    (optional)

Makes about ½ cup

anchovy vinaigrette

(pictured top left on opposite page)

5 anchovies in olive oil,
    mashed with the side
    of a knife
1 teaspoon finely grated
    orange zest
2 teaspoons Dijon mustard
2 teaspoons apple cider
    vinegar
½ teaspoon honey
¼ cup extra-virgin olive oil
Sea salt and freshly ground
    black pepper

Makes about ½ cup

honey balsamic dressing

(pictured top right on opposite page)

¼ cup extra-virgin olive oil
2 tablespoons balsamic vinegar
1 teaspoon Dijon mustard
1 teaspoon honey
Sea salt and freshly ground
    black pepper

Makes about ½ cup

naked dressing

1 teaspoon grainy mustard
¼ cup freshly squeezed orange
    juice
¼ cup extra-virgin olive oil
Sea salt and freshly ground
    black pepper

Makes about ½ cup

homemade ghee

(pictured bottom left on opposite page)

2 cups (1 pound) butter

1 Sterilize a 2-cup canning jar and its lid by setting them in a saucepan filled with enough water to submerge them. Bring the water to a boil, then drain and let the jar and lid dry completely before using.

2 Heat the butter in a saucepan over low heat. Once completely melted, simmer for 15 to 25 minutes, skimming off any froth that rises to the surface, until the milk solids begin to separate and sink to the bottom of the pan.

3 Remove from the heat and let cool for 15 minutes, then pour through a fine-mesh strainer or cheesecloth-lined strainer to remove the milk solids (discard these) into the sterilized jar. Store in the refrigerator for up to 6 months.

Makes about 1½ cups

pure raw stripped bare nude clean detox

molasses + ginger porkballs with bok choy

Baked meatballs are a bit of a revelation; they acheive a pleasing oven-roasted crispness on top, but they are soft and mouthwateringly tender underneath.

1 pound, 2 ounces ground pork
2 cups fresh rye or spelt bread crumbs
3 garlic cloves, minced
1 tablespoon grated fresh ginger
Finely grated zest of 1 lemon
1 heaping teaspoon spicy smoked paprika
2 tablespoons minced cilantro sprigs
1 tablespoon blackstrap molasses
1 tablespoon honey
1 heaping teaspoon sea salt
Freshly ground black pepper
1 tablespoon coconut oil, plus more for cooking bok choy
2½ to 3½ cups chicken stock (page 8)
4 baby bok choy, halved

Serves 2 to 3

1 Preheat the oven to 400°F.

2 Put the ground pork, bread crumbs, garlic, ginger, lemon zest, and paprika in a mixing bowl. Add the cilantro, molasses, honey, salt, and a little pepper. Using your hands, mix together well and then form the mixture into 12 to 14 patties.

3 Heat the oil in a large skillet, then fry the patties until brown on both sides. Place in a shallow ovenproof dish and add enough stock to come three-quarters of the way up the patties. Bake for 15 minutes.

4 Meanwhile, heat a little oil in the pan used to cook the patties. Add the bok choy, sliced side down, and fry for a couple of minutes until golden and soft, adding 1 tablespoon of water halfway through to prevent burning.

5 Ladle the porkballs and cooking liquid into shallow bowls, add the bok choy and a grinding of pepper, and serve.

bacon, cabbage + pearl barley broth

This simple, quick recipe is filling and cheap, as well as an ideal way to use up leftovers. The key is to use high-quality, strong-flavored stock, preferably homemade. If you are short of time, you can use the cheaty precooked packages of pearl barley or mixed grains that are available in most grocery stores; just wash them first.

1 cup pearl barley
Sea salt
7 ounces smoked
 bacon, diced
1 onion, minced
1 large celery stalk, sliced
 (save the leaves for
 garnish)
4 garlic cloves, chopped
3 cups chicken stock
 (page 8)
½ small red cabbage,
 shredded
Freshly ground black
 pepper
Small handful of flat-leaf
 parsley leaves
Freshly squeezed lemon
 juice, to taste
¼ cup lightly toasted
 slivered almonds,
 for garnish

Serves 4

1 Put the barley in a large saucepan, cover with cold water, add a big pinch of salt, and bring to a boil. Decrease the heat to low, cover, and simmer until the barley is tender, 30 to 40 minutes. Drain well and return to the pan.

2 Meanwhile, cook the bacon pieces in a skillet over high heat for 5 minutes, then add the onion and celery. Decrease the heat and gently sauté until soft. Add the garlic and cook for a couple of minutes, then add the contents of the skillet to the pan with the drained barley.

3 Add the stock and bring to a boil, then decrease the heat and add the cabbage. Simmer for about 10 minutes, until the cabbage has softened but still retains texture and crunch. Season with salt and pepper to taste.

4 Stir in the parsley and a good squeeze of lemon juice. Ladle into bowls and enjoy hot, with a few celery leaves and a sprinkle of slivered almonds on top.

hot + spicy seafood soup with crispy shallots

This dish is a quicker, Thai fish–inspired version of my mother's magic, spicy coconut soup. It's warming, restorative, and healing, with an added kick from chile, zesty lime, lemongrass, and ginger to clear the pipes and heat the belly.

2 tablespoons coconut oil
3 shallots, finely sliced
Generous 2 cups chicken stock (page 8) or fish stock (page 9)
1¼ cups canned coconut milk
1 heaping tablespoon tom yum paste
1-inch piece of fresh ginger, grated
2 large fresh Kaffir lime leaves, or 4 dried
2 lemongrass stalks, smashed
2¾ ounces shiitake mushrooms, chopped
1 baby bok choy, halved
7 ounces frozen mixed seafood, such as prawns, mussels, and squid rings, defrosted
2 tablespoons freshly squeezed lime juice
2 tablespoons fish sauce
2 to 3 teaspoons coconut palm sugar
1 to 2 red chiles, sliced
Fresh cilantro leaves

Serves 2

1 Heat the coconut oil in a small skillet, add the shallots, and fry over high heat until crispy, then drain and set aside.

2 Put the stock and coconut milk in a pan with the tom yum paste, ginger, lime leaves, and lemongrass. Bring to a boil, then add the mushrooms, bok choy, and seafood.

3 Simmer for about 1 minute, until the prawns start to turn pink; any longer than that and they will overcook. Season with the lime juice, fish sauce, and palm sugar to taste. Ladle into bowls, removing the lemongrass. Sprinkle with the crispy shallots, chiles, and cilantro leaves and serve.

smoked haddock in coconut milk

This is a surprisingly fresh dish, despite the rich taste that often occurs in dishes using smoked fish. I vary between serving it as a soup, as it is here, and as a fish entrée, with a thicker sauce made by reducing the coconut liquid by a quarter once the cooked fish has been plated up.

2 smoked haddock fillets,
   8 ounces each
½ onion
2 bay leaves
2 cloves
Scant 1 cup dry white wine
1¾ cups canned coconut
   milk
Sea salt
1 tablespoon coconut oil
3½ ounces baby spinach
1 to 2 tablespoons
   tarragon leaves
Pink peppercorns,
   for garnish

Serves 2

1 Put the haddock fillets in a large skillet with the onion, bay leaves, and cloves. Add the wine and coconut milk and poach gently until the fish flakes easily when tested with a fork, about 7 minutes. Using a large spatula, remove the fillets to a plate and cover with foil to keep warm. Skim the cooking liquid to remove any scum, add salt to taste, then strain through a strainer and keep hot.

2 Melt the coconut oil in another pan and add the spinach. Cook until wilted, then drain well. Divide the wilted spinach between 2 warmed serving bowls and top with the haddock, flaking it a little as you do so. Ladle the broth on top and sprinkle with tarragon. Garnish with pink peppercorns and serve immediately.

yoga bowl

This is the sort of restorative dish that your body yearns for after exercise. It is packed full of natural plant-based protein, including beta-carotene-rich sweet potato and nutty brown rice. This is pure comfort in a bowl.

1¼ cups red lentils
2 tablespoons coconut oil
1 onion, minced
4 garlic cloves, crushed
1-inch piece of fresh ginger
2 teaspoons cumin seeds
1 tablespoon mild curry
   powder
Pinch of sea salt
5 cups vegetable stock
Scant 1 cup canned
   coconut milk
9 ounces sweet potato,
   peeled and cubed
Freshly ground black
   pepper
Cooked brown rice,
   for serving
Coconut Salsa (page 12),
   for serving

Serves 4

1 Wash the lentils until the water runs clear, then drain and put in a large pan.

2 Heat the oil in a skillet over low heat, add the onion, and sauté until soft. Add the garlic, ginger, cumin seeds, and curry powder and cook, stirring occasionally, for a couple of minutes to bring out their fragrance.

3 Add the onion and spices to the lentils with a pinch of salt. Stir in the stock and coconut milk. Bring to a boil and skim off any scum that rises to the surface.

4 Turn down the heat and simmer very gently, with the lid ajar, for 25 to 30 minutes, until creamy, stirring occasionally. Add the sweet potato and cook for 10 to 15 minutes, uncovered, until the sweet potato is soft but not falling apart. Add a little water if necessary to achieve the preferred consistency, and season with pepper and more salt to taste.

5 Serve with a scoop of brown rice and a dollop of coconut salsa.

chilled avocado + yogurt soup

Swirl a little bit of tahini with a dollop of yogurt with live cultures for the ultimate naked springtime soup.

Flesh of 2 large avocados
3 garlic cloves
8 green onions
3 tablespoons mint leaves
3 tablespoons cilantro
   leaves
1¾ cups chilled vegetable
   stock
Scant 1 cup plain yogurt
   with live cultures, plus
   more for serving
Juice of 1 lemon
Sea salt and a good
   grinding of fresh
   black pepper
Tahini Dressing (page 17),
   for serving

Serves 4 as an appetizer

1 Put the avocado, garlic, green onions, mint, cilantro, vegetable stock, and yogurt in a blender and blend to a fine, smooth puree. Stir in the lemon juice to taste, then season with salt and pepper. Chill well. Ladle into bowls and add a swirl of the tahini dressing and yogurt.

pure **raw** stripped bare nude clean detox

sauerkraut

Invest in intestinal bacteria today; only half an hour of work and you will have a wonderful supply of natural probiotics at your disposal for months. Made from nothing more than cabbage and salt, and any other spices and aromatics you fancy, it is a bit of a pickle to make, but worth it, as it keeps for ages. Mix it into grains or dollop it on stews.

1 red cabbage
1½ tablespoons fine
sea salt
1 tablespoon caraway
seeds

Makes about 2 quarts

1 Cut the cabbage into quarters and trim out the core. Slice each quarter down its length, making 8 wedges. Slice each wedge crosswise into very thin ribbons.

2 Transfer the cabbage to a large bowl and sprinkle with the salt and caraway seeds. Using your hands, work them into the cabbage by massaging and squeezing the cabbage for 10 minutes.

3 Weigh the cabbage down with a plate slightly smaller than the bowl and place a heavy object on the plate. Cover the bowl with a cloth and secure it with a rubber band or twine. This allows air to flow in and out, but not dust or insects.

4 Let ferment at cool room temperature (64°F to 75°F) away from direct sunlight for 7 to 10 days, pressing down on the plate every so often during the first 48 hours. Check it daily and press it down if the cabbage is floating above the liquid.

5 Transfer to sterilized, dry jars (see the ghee recipe on page 17) and store for several months. It will keep even longer if refrigerated. As long as it still tastes and smells good to eat, it will be.

kimchi

This is a traditional spicy and sour condiment made from fermented cabbage and a variety of punchy, strong spices. It is also known for being beneficial for digestive health, and full of vitamins A, B, and C. I use it alongside slippery, sesame-dressed noodles, or simply mixed into steamed brown rice, with some tamari and a fried egg.

1 large Chinese cabbage
⅔ cup coarse sea salt
3½ quarts water
1 head of garlic, peeled and minced
2-inch piece of fresh ginger, peeled and minced
¼ cup fish sauce
4 tablespoons ground chiles
1 bunch of green onions, cut into 1¼-inch lengths
1 teaspoon honey

Makes about 2 quarts

1 Cut the cabbage in half lengthwise, then slice each half lengthwise into 3 sections. Cut away the tough stem parts.

2 Dissolve the salt in the water in a very large container, then submerge the cabbage in the water. Put a plate on top to keep it submerged and let stand for 2 hours.

3 Mix the remaining ingredients in a very large metal or glass bowl. Drain the cabbage, rinse it, and squeeze it dry.

4 Here's the scary part: use your hands to mix it all up (wear rubber gloves as the ground chiles can stain your hands). Pack into a sterilized jar large enough to hold it all (see the ghee recipe on page 17) and cover tightly. Let stand for 1 to 2 days at cool room temperature (64°F to 75°F).

5 Check the kimchi: If it's bubbling a bit, it's fermenting and ready to be refrigerated. If not, let it stand another day, after which it should be ready. Once it's fermenting, serve or store in the refrigerator, and eat within 3 weeks.

beef carpaccio with capers + arugula

There is something unsurpassably good about the simplicity of carpaccio. The salty capers, fruity olive oil, and zesty lemon combined together turn this simple, soft meat into something spectacular.

1 pound beef top round
Sea salt
Big handful of arugula
¼ cup extra-virgin olive oil
Finely grated zest and juice
of ½ lemon
2 tablespoons small
capers, rinsed and
coarsely chopped
Freshly ground black
pepper

Serves 4

1 Put the beef in the freezer for 30 to 45 minutes. When it is firm and partly frozen, take it out and, using a very sharp knife, carefully cut it into thin slices.

2 Place about 4 slices of beef on a large silicone baking mat, spaced well apart. Place a second silicone mat on top and pound with a rolling pin until the slices have expanded and thinned. You are looking to get them to about the thickness of a strand of spaghetti.

3 Peel off the top silicone mat, then peel off the slices of beef. Repeat the pounding process with the remaining slices. Season each slice with a little salt, wrap in plastic wrap, and refrigerate for up to 12 hours.

4 When ready to serve, put the arugula in a bowl and dress with a pinch of salt and a little of the olive oil and lemon juice. Divide the beef between 4 plates, or serve on a large platter. Sprinkle with the capers and dress with the remaining lemon juice and zest, olive oil, and a generous grinding of pepper. Add a handful of arugula to each plate and serve immediately.

salmon tartare + wasabi crème fraîche

If you are new to eating fish raw, then this wicked dish is a good place to start. It works as an appetizer but is also great piled up in an avocado boat (see page 38). The wasabi is pretty punchy, so if it is too strong, just add another tablespoon of crème fraîche.

2 very fresh salmon fillets, about 10½ ounces in total
¼ cucumber
1 tablespoon capers, rinsed and thoroughly dried
3 heaping tablespoons fresh dill weed
½ teaspoon lemon zest
Freshly squeezed lemon juice
1 tablespoon extra-virgin olive oil
Generous grinding of black pepper
Wasabi Crème Fraîche (page 12), for serving

Serves 2 as a main course, or 4 as an appetizer

1 If the salmon fillets have the skin on, remove it but don't throw it away (see Crispy Salmon Skin, below). Cut the salmon into ¼-inch cubes. Cut the cucumber the same size or a little smaller. Coarsely chop the capers and dill.

2 Put the salmon in a large bowl with the capers, cucumber, dill, lemon zest and juice, and olive oil and toss to combine. Press half of the mixture into a greased ramekin, using the back of a spoon to compress it. Place a plate over the ramekin and invert. Remove the ramekin and repeat with the remaining mixture and a second plate. Dollop on the crème fraîche, grind some pepper over the top, and serve.

crispy salmon skin

Rub a pinch of salt onto each side of the salmon skin. Heat a dry nonstick skillet over medium-high heat, add the skin, and cook for about 5 minutes on each side, until golden and crispy. When it snaps easily, it's ready. Serve with the salmon tartare or eat it as a healthy snack.

avocado boats with peas, feta + mint

Handy for speedy meals, this pea mixture can be prepared in a double quantity and kept in the refrigerator to make this recipe even quicker. Just pop it in a lunch box with some salad greens, grab an avocado, and you have yourself a convenient desk lunch.

1 cup frozen peas
½ cup crumbled feta,
    plus more for garnish
1 garlic clove, crushed
2 tablespoons freshly
    squeezed lime juice,
    plus more for garnish
2 tablespoons chopped
    mint leaves, plus more
    for garnish
2 tablespoons extra-virgin
    olive oil, plus more for
    garnish
2 avocados
Freshly ground black
    pepper

Serves 2

1 Roughly blend the peas, feta, garlic, lime juice, mint, and oil together in a blender. Alternatively, let the peas thaw and mash the ingredients together using a fork to a rough texture. If it's too thick, add a little more olive oil or lime juice.

2 Slice the avocados in half, remove the pits, and score a few crisscross slits into the flesh. Pile the pea puree high into each half. Add a generous grinding of pepper and a little extra feta, olive oil, lime juice, and mint leaves.

dill cucumber pickle

The perfect way to eat pickled cucumbers is to serve them with cooked oily fish. The combination makes for a powerful taste sensation.

1½ **pounds small**
   cucumbers (about 5)
2 cups water
2 cups apple cider vinegar
3 tablespoons fine sea salt
8 dill sprigs
8 garlic cloves, peeled

Makes about 4 cups

1 Wash and dry the cucumbers, remove the ends, and cut into thick sticks.

2 Put the water, vinegar, and salt in a pan and boil for 10 minutes.

3 Pack the cucumbers, dill, and garlic evenly into warm, sterilized jars (see the ghee recipe on page 17) and pour in the pickling liquid, ensuring the cucumbers are covered. Top off with water if need be.

4 Seal the jars with their lids and gently tap the jars against the counter a few times to remove all the air bubbles. Store at room temperature or in the refrigerator for up to 6 months. Wait at least 2 to 3 days before eating to allow time for the flavors to infuse. Once opened, they will keep for a couple of weeks in the refrigerator.

raw spring rolls +
peanut dipping sauce

A rainbow of colorful shredded veggies, rice paper wrappers, and a mega chunky peanut dipping sauce are all it takes for these tasty spring rolls to sing. For anyone cutting out carbohydrates, I recommend steamed cabbage leaves or raw lettuce leaves instead of rice paper wrappers.

4 cups mixed fresh vegetables (such as bell pepper, radishes, cucumber, carrot, bean sprouts, celery, kohlrabi, green onions, and avocado)

6 to 8 rice paper wrappers (4-inch circles or larger)

1 teaspoon chopped red chile

Handful of fresh herbs, (such as mint, basil, and cilantro)

A few edible flowers (optional, but they look pretty through the wrapper)

Chunky Peanut Dipping Sauce (page 15), for serving

Serves 2

1 Prepare the vegetables separately, cutting them into julienne, sticks, or thin circles as appropriate. Fill a large bowl with warm water. Quickly dip each rice paper wrapper in the water for 10 to 15 seconds, until soft but not falling apart.

2 Place the wet wrappers on a clean counter. Arrange the prepared vegetables, chile, herbs, and flowers on each rice wrapper, about a third of the way up. Tuck in the sides and roll. The trick is to not overpack them.

3 Serve immediately with the dipping sauce, either whole, or cut in half for a quick bite.

sea bass ceviche with avocado + pomegranate

Although the fish gets cold "cooked" by the citrus juice, it is still raw, so buying fresh, sushi-grade fish is essential for ceviche. The creamy avocado works as a perfect counterpoint to the fresh pop of the pomegranate and the zesty lime-licked fish.

**9 ounces skinless,
    boneless sea bass
    or sea bream fillets**
½ teaspoon sea salt
Juice of 3 limes
1 green chile, finely sliced
**Small handful of cilantro
    leaves, coarsely chopped**
**½ small avocado, diced,
    for garnish**
**2 to 3 tablespoons
    pomegranate seeds,
    for garnish**
**2 green onions, finely
    sliced, for garnish**

Serves 2

1 Cut the fish into thin slices and rub with the salt. Spread out in a shallow dish and leave for 1 minute, then pour in the lime juice, sprinkle with the chile, and let marinate for 15 minutes. If there is a lot of liquid, drain a little away, then mix in the cilantro. Check the seasoning and adjust if necessary.

2 Garnish with the avocado, pomegranate seeds, and green onions and serve.

Tip
In order to get the pomegranate seeds out of their shell without too much mess, you can submerge the pomegranate halves in a bowl of water before breaking them apart.

mackerel ceviche in ponzu sauce

Ponzu is a citrusy soy sauce, which works in perfect balance with oily mackerel. Fresh, sushi-grade fish is essential for this recipe. Serve cool, but not refrigerator-cold, as a simple appetizer, or with steamed bok choy and sticky brown rice for a more substantial meal.

5-ounce sushi-grade mackerel, filleted and pin bones removed, skin on

Generous ⅓ cup tamari

¼ cup freshly squeezed orange juice

1 tablespoon freshly squeezed lime juice

1 tablespoon rice vinegar

½ red Thai chile, thinly sliced, for garnish

A few fresh mint leaves, minced, for garnish

1 to 2 tablespoons toasted sesame seeds, for garnish

Serves 2

1 Wash and dry the mackerel gently but thoroughly. Mix the tamari, orange juice, lime juice, and vinegar in a bowl. Strain through a strainer and set aside. Slice the mackerel into pieces ½ to ¾ inch thick.

2 If eating immediately, serve the mackerel slices sitting in a pool of the sauce sprinkled with the chile, mint, and sesame seeds. If serving later, store the fish and sauce separately in the refrigerator. When ready to serve, let both warm for a bit at room temperature before plating.

tomatoes with capers, almonds + herbs

My all-time fave salad, inspired by the colors and flavors of Istanbul. I tend to use heirloom tomatoes for variety, but you could use a mixture of ripe cherry and plum tomatoes as well.

1 pound, 2 ounces mixed
  variety tomatoes
3 tablespoons extra-virgin
  olive oil
1 tablespoon maple syrup
1 tablespoon freshly
  squeezed lemon juice
½ teaspoon spicy smoked
  paprika
1 small shallot,
  finely chopped
2 tablespoons small
  capers, rinsed and
  coarsely chopped
⅓ cup smoked almonds,
  coarsely chopped
Small handful of flat-leaf
  parsley, chopped
Sea salt and freshly
  ground black pepper

Serves 4 to 6

1 Slice the tomatoes into a mixture of disks and wedges; different sizes and shapes are nice for variation.

2 Mix the olive oil, maple syrup, lemon juice, and smoked paprika in a bowl.

3 Add the shallot, capers, tomatoes, half of the almonds, and three-quarters of the parsley and mix well. Season with salt and pepper to taste and serve topped with the remaining parsley and almonds.

ribboned kale + nectarine salad

This is my healthy coleslaw alternative. Serve it with anything from broiled meats to grain-based salads. Or eat it with a fried egg on top and a handful of toasted seeds.

5 ounces kale
¼ small red cabbage
⅙ small green cabbage
Very large handful of chopped parsley or cilantro
2 nectarines, quartered and sliced
1 to 2 tablespoons toasted sesame seeds, to taste
Tamari Dressing (page 17)

Serves 4

1 Fill a large bowl with ice and water. Place a steamer over a pan of simmering water. Wash and dry the kale and remove the stalks, then finely slice into long, thin shreds. Cut both cabbages into long thin shreds, removing the large stalks.

2 Place all the cabbage and the kale in the steamer and steam for 1 to 2 minutes to soften slightly and remove bitterness, tossing gently halfway through to ensure even steaming. Remove from the heat and plunge into the iced water to preserve their vibrant color.

3 Drain and dry well and place in a large dish or on a platter. Add the parsley and nectarine slices and toss together gently. Sprinkle with the sesame seeds and drizzle with the dressing.

Tip
If preparing this salad ahead, you can dress the kale and cabbage in advance and avoid having to steam them first; the dressing will help soften and break them down, making them less fibrous.

green cauliflower "couscous" with pumpkin seeds

This vibrant green dish is so versatile and can act as a stand-alone salad or as a rice substitute. I often swap the cheese for broiled chicken and use edamame or green beans rather than fava beans.

1 head cauliflower, stem and florets coarsely chopped

3 tablespoons extra-virgin olive oil, plus more for serving

2 garlic cloves, chopped

7 ounces thawed frozen, or cooked fresh, fava beans

½ cup pumpkin seeds, lightly toasted

2 handfuls of mixed herbs (such as mint and basil), minced

2 tablespoons freshly squeezed lemon juice

Scant ½ cup crumbled soft goat cheese

Sea salt and freshly ground black pepper

Serves 4

1 Put the cauliflower in a food processor and process to a fine couscous- or ricelike texture, in batches if you have a small food processor.

2 Heat 2 tablespoons of the olive oil in a large skillet, add the garlic, and cook, stirring occasionally, until lightly golden. Add the cauliflower, tossing it to coat with the garlic oil. Cook, stirring occasionally, for about 5 minutes, until heated through. Transfer to a large serving bowl.

3 Add the fava beans, pumpkin seeds, herbs, lemon juice, goat cheese, and remaining 1 tablespoon of olive oil. Toss until mixed. Season with salt and pepper to taste and finish with a drizzle of olive oil. Serve warm.

summer salad bowl

The greens I use for this vary depending on the season. In summer, it will be composed of raw salad greens, so the steaming might only be for a few green beans or a little chard, whereas in the winter, when I feel the need for warmth, more of the greens (broccoli, Tuscan kale, and kale) will be steamed. The tahini dressing works superbly, although there are many other options (see page 17).

12 asparagus spears, woody ends broken off, or a handful of green beans
1 cup fresh peas
1 small head broccoli, broken into florets
Big handful of kale, chard, or spinach
1 head baby Boston lettuce, for serving
Tahini Dressing (page 17)
½ cup watercress leaves, for serving
1 tablespoon chopped chives or cilantro, for serving

Serves 2 to 4

1 Fill a large bowl with ice and water. Place a steamer over a pan of simmering water.

2 Steam the vegetables one type at a time to avoid overcooking—when still crunchy, vegetables retain more of their goodness and are more pleasing in texture. Steam asparagus for 4 to 8 minutes, depending on thickness; green beans and peas for 2 to 3 minutes; broccoli florets for 2 to 4 minutes; and kale, chard, or spinach for 1 to 2 minutes.

3 Once cooked, plunge the steamed vegetables into the iced water (this will help retain their crispness and vibrant green color); or, if you wish to serve them hot, simply omit this step. Place the steamed vegetables in a serving bowl with the lettuce and watercress. Drizzle with tahini dressing and sprinkle the herbs on top.

green bean, almond +
sheep cheese salad

This quick dish is another one of my favorite salads. The sweetness of the dried cranberries, the crunchy green beans, and the salty cheese all work wonderfully together. Although this would work as a side for four, you can eat it as an entrée for two, with a few more handfuls of arugula, extra slivered almonds, and more crumbled cheese.

14 ounces green beans, trimmed
¼ cup extra-virgin olive oil
1 to 2 tablespoons freshly squeezed lemon juice, to taste
Large handful of arugula
Small handful of parsley leaves
⅔ cup slivered almonds, toasted
¾ cup crumbled feta cheese
¼ chopped dried cranberries
Sea salt and freshly ground black pepper

Serves 4 as an appetizer, or 2 as a main course

1 Bring a pan of water to a boil, add the beans and cook, covered, for 3 to 4 minutes, until tender to the bite but still snappable and vibrant green. Drain in a colander and run cold water over them until cool.

2 Meanwhile, put the olive oil and lemon juice in a large bowl and whisk well.

3 Add the cooled beans, arugula, parsley, almonds, feta, and cranberries to the dressing and toss to combine. Season to taste with salt and pepper, then serve.

endive, egg + olive salad

A light, fresh, and simple dish for a speedy meal. You can also make it more substantial by serving it with cooked grains, such as spelt, pearl barley, or wild rice.

2 eggs, at room
    temperature
2 heads endive,
    leaves separated
⅓ cup Kalamata olives,
    pits removed
¼ cup Naked Dressing
    (page 17)
Sea salt and freshly ground
    black pepper

Serves 2

1 Bring a large pan of water to a boil. When large bubbles are breaking on the surface, remove from the heat and quickly but gently lower in the eggs one at a time, using a spoon. Return to the heat and boil for 6 to 7 minutes, depending on the size of the eggs.

2 Meanwhile, arrange the endive leaves on 2 plates. Halve the olives and sprinkle them over each plate.

3 Drain the eggs and run cold water over them until cool enough to handle. Peel and quarter each egg and divide the quarters between the plates.

4 Drizzle a couple of tablespoons of the dressing over each and season with salt and pepper to taste.

soba noodle salad with cucumber + mango

This is undoubtedly best served cold and packed up for desktop lunches or picnics. For a more substantial main dish, add some grilled shrimp. They work wonders with the sweet mango and the earthy sesame dressing. For another option, try it topped with a soft boiled egg; the yolk on the noodles adds a deep, creamy richness to the dressing. Note that you'll need a double recipe of the Tamari Dressing for this dish.

7 ounces soba noodles
1 cup Tamari Dressing
   (page 17)
1 small cucumber, cut into
   fine strips
½ large green mango,
   cut into fine strips
4 green onions,
   finely sliced
1 large green chile,
   minced
2 tablespoons black
   sesame seeds
Small handful of cilantro
   leaves, chopped

Serves 4

1 Bring a large pan of water to a boil and add the soba noodles. When the water returns to a boil, add a cup of cold water, then repeat when the water comes to a boil again. Simmer vigorously for 4 to 5 minutes, until the noodles are still slightly al dente. Drain and rinse well under cold water, then place in a bowl and cover with cold water to prevent the noodles from getting sticky.

2 When ready to serve, drain the noodles and place in a bowl. Add half of the dressing, the cucumber, mango, green onions, chile, and most of the sesame seeds and cilantro. Taste and adjust the dressing and seasoning.

3 Arrange on a platter or in individual bowls, top with the remaining sesame seeds and cilantro, and serve with the remaining dressing alongside.

Tip
If making ahead, mix 1 teaspoon of olive oil into the dish to prevent the noodles from sticking, and keep the dressing separate. Mix the dressing in just before eating.

calamari with chile, lemon + celery salt

This is an economical, no-oil-wasted recipe. It is more virtuous than its deep-fried counterpart but just as delicious, with a pleasing crunch from the cornmeal. If you can't find fine cornmeal, just process a coarser one for a few seconds in a food processor. Best served with a simple salad.

1 pound, 2 ounces
   calamari, washed and
   prepared
A little milk (optional)
2 eggs
1 cup fine cornmeal
2 teaspoons red pepper
   flakes
Finely grated zest of
   4 lemons
1 heaping teaspoon
   celery salt
Coconut oil, for shallow
   frying
Sea salt flakes, for serving
Lemon wedges, for serving

Serves 2

1 If the calamari is super fresh, there is no need to soak it. Otherwise, soak it in milk for 30 minutes to tenderize. Drain and slice the calamari into rings about ½ inch thick. Trim the tentacles if you are using slightly larger calamari.

2 Briefly whisk the eggs in a bowl. Put the cornmeal, red pepper flakes, lemon zest, and celery salt in another bowl and mix well .

3 Dry the calamari rings thoroughly, then dip each ring into the beaten egg, then into the cornmeal mixture to coat. Set aside on a plate lined with paper towels. If you have enough cornmeal and egg, you can dip the calamari again.

4 Heat a ½-inch depth of oil in a deep skillet and fry the calamari in batches for 3 to 4 minutes, until the crust is crisp and golden and the calamari is white throughout. Turn over during cooking and be careful not to overcook or the calamari will become tough. Top off with oil as needed; the idea is to keep a little in the bottom to prevent sticking, but not to swamp the pan.

5 Once each batch is cooked, transfer to another plate lined with paper towels to drain any excess oil. Serve hot, sprinkled with sea salt flakes and with lemon wedges alongside.

sea bass, squash + quinoa

You can use any firm white fish for this and any type of quinoa you fancy—the black just makes for a beautiful color contrast against the delicate fish, vibrant squash puree, and sage leaves. Roasting the squash intensifies the flavor, but if you are short on time you can steam it.

½ butternut squash (9 to 12 ounces), peeled
6 tablespoons coconut oil
Sea salt and freshly ground black pepper
⅔ cup black quinoa
2½ cups chicken stock (page 8) or vegetable stock
1 small onion, minced
2 garlic cloves, minced
8 large sage leaves, 4 chopped
2 sea bass fillets (about 5 ounces each), or other firm white fish
Lemon wedges, for serving

Serves 2

1 Preheat the oven to 400°F. Cut the squash into half-moon slices and spread out on a baking sheet. Melt 1 tablespoon of the coconut oil in a small skillet, then drizzle it over the squash. Season the squash with salt and pepper, and bake for 30 to 40 minutes, until tender.

2 Meanwhile, toast the quinoa in a pan for 5 to 10 minutes, until it's nutty brown and starts to pop. Add 1¼ cups of the stock. Bring to a boil, then decrease the heat, cover, and simmer for 15 to 20 minutes, until the liquid is absorbed.

3 Melt 1 tablespoon of the coconut oil in a small skillet, add the onion, and sauté until translucent. Stir in the garlic and chopped sage. Cook for 2 minutes, then transfer to a blender with the squash, 1 tablespoon of the coconut oil, and enough of the remaining stock to blend the mixture to a thick paste.

4 Melt 2 tablespoons of the coconut oil in the same small skillet until hot, then fry the 4 whole sage leaves until crispy.

5 Season the fillets. Melt the remaining 1 tablespoon of coconut oil in a large skillet until hot. Add the fillets and cook for 2 to 3 minutes on each side, until the flesh is opaque.

6 Divide the squash purée between 2 plates. Top with a mound of quinoa, then a fillet. Add a squeeze of lemon juice and a couple of fried sage leaves to each, and serve.

Hainanese chicken

I was introduced to this dish by an ex-boyfriend, who used to feed it to me when I was ill. Made up of four main components—chicken, broth, cabbage, and rice—it is one of the simplest and cleanest dishes. I recommend white basmati as it really soaks up the flavor of the broth, but brown rice works too. Traditionally, the meal would begin with the cabbage and broth, with the chicken and rice for mains, but it can be eaten all together in one course too.

1 chicken (4 to 4½ pounds)
Small bunch of cilantro
1-inch piece whole fresh ginger, plus ¼-inch piece fresh ginger, chopped
2 teaspoons sea salt, plus more for serving
1 tablespoon coconut oil
6 garlic cloves, chopped
1½ cups basmati rice
1 small cabbage, shredded
Freshly ground black pepper
1 to 2 red chiles, finely sliced
Tamari, for serving

Serves 6

1 Put the chicken in a large Dutch oven or pan and add enough water to cover. Separate the cilantro leaves from the stems and set aside the leaves. Tie the stems together with string and add to the pan, along with the whole piece of ginger and the salt.

2 Bring to a boil, then decrease the heat, cover, and simmer for 50 minutes, skimming off any scum that rises to the surface.

3 Meanwhile, heat the coconut oil in a small skillet over medium heat and add the chopped ginger and garlic. Fry until light golden and crispy, then set aside.

4 Carefully transfer the cooked chicken to a bowl, cover, and set aside. Remove the cilantro and ginger and reserve the poaching liquid. Wash the rice in a strainer under cold water, then add it to the poaching liquid. Simmer over medium heat for 15 to 20 minutes, until tender. Add the cabbage 3 to 4 minutes before the end of the rice's cooking time. When the cabbage is tender, spoon it into a bowl with some poaching liquid and season with salt and pepper to taste.

5 Shred the chicken into large strips. Serve the cabbage and broth, then the chicken and strained rice, with the chiles, cilantro leaves, crispy ginger and garlic, and tamari as garnishes.

bloody Mary mussels

The spicy, smoky tomato sauce works wonders for fresh mussels. If you don't fancy making your own smoky tomato juice, go for a store-bought brand and pimp it up.

2¼ pounds mussels, debearded and rinsed in cold water

2 tablespoons extra-virgin olive oil, plus more for drizzling

1 celery stalk, finely chopped (save the leaves for garnish)

4 garlic cloves, crushed

2 tablespoons tomato paste

Generous 2 cups Smoky Bloody Mary juice (see page 110; omit the vodka and celery stalks), or any good-quality store-bought tomato juice

6 cherry tomatoes, halved and seeded

Sea salt and freshly ground black pepper

Serves 4

1 Scrub and carefully check the mussels to be sure all are closed (discard any that are open). Soak the mussels in cold water for 20 to 30 minutes to release any impurities, then drain.

2 Heat the olive oil over medium-high heat in a large saucepan or sauté pan wide enough so the mussels won't pile up on top of each other.

3 Add the celery and sauté for 5 minutes, then add the garlic and stir until fragrant, about 1 minute. Stir in the tomato paste and cook for a minute or two, then add the tomato juice and cherry tomatoes. Stir well and cook for another 1 to 2 minutes, until bubbling. Meanwhile, chop the celery leaves and set aside.

4 Add the mussels to the pan, cover, and cook for 2 minutes. Check, and if they are mostly closed, continue cooking for another 2 minutes, checking every minute until they are mostly opened. Discard any that haven't opened. Taste the sauce and season with salt and pepper, then drizzle with a little olive oil, top with the celery leaves, and serve hot.

miso salmon

If you can get your hands on lightly smoked salmon, it is delicious in this recipe. The smoky flavor of the fish complements the sweet and salty miso beautifully. I like to serve it with a shaved vegetable salad and Tamari Dressing (page 17), or with steamed rice and Kimchi (page 33).

½ **cup white miso**
¼ **cup mirin or sweet**
white wine
2 **tablespoons unseasoned**
rice vinegar
2 **to 3 tablespoons tamari,**
to taste
1½ **tablespoons finely**
chopped fresh ginger
2 **teaspoons toasted**
sesame oil
4 **salmon fillets,**
8 ounces each
Sea salt and freshly ground
black pepper

Serves 4

1 Whisk together the miso, mirin, vinegar, tamari, ginger, and sesame oil in a small bowl. Place the salmon fillets side by side in a baking dish, pour in the marinade, and turn to coat. Cover and marinate for at least 30 and up to 60 minutes in the refrigerator.

2 Preheat the broiler. Remove the salmon from the marinade and season with salt and pepper. Place under the broiler with the door open, skin side down, and cook until golden brown and a crust has formed, 3 to 4 minutes.

3 Turn the salmon over and cook for 3 to 4 minutes more; you want the salmon to retain its plump pinkness in the center. Season with plenty of pepper and serve.

lamb meatballs with rhubarb sauce

The combination of lamb and rhubarb is an unusual but delicious one. The rhubarb is laced with the heady notes of cardamom, cumin, and cinnamon, and simmered low and slow, it turns into more of a rich spiced jam than a sauce. Pair the fragrant meatballs with brown rice, and you will have a table of happy diners.

For the meatballs:
1 pound, 2 ounces lean ground lamb
1 onion, very finely chopped
2 garlic cloves, crushed
½ teaspoon cayenne pepper
1 teaspoon ground cinnamon
1 teaspoon ground cumin
1 teaspoon sea salt
1 teaspoon black pepper
1 small egg, beaten
1 tablespoon coconut oil

For the rhubarb sauce:
1 cup chicken stock (page 8)
10½ ounces rhubarb, cut into 3-inch lengths
4 cardamom pods, crushed
¼ cup date syrup
½ teaspoon ground cumin
½ teaspoon ground cinnamon
Sea salt
Scant 1 cup water

For serving:
Steamed brown rice
⅓ cup pistachios, chopped
Handful of cilantro leaves

1 To make the meatballs, mix the lamb, onion, garlic, cayenne, cinnamon, cumin, salt, and pepper in a bowl, then mix in the egg. Cover with plastic wrap and let rest for 30 minutes in the refrigerator, then shape the mixture into about 20 balls.

2 Heat the coconut oil in a large skillet. Fry the meatballs in batches, about 5 at a time, until nicely browned on all sides and cooked almost through to the middle, then set aside and keep warm. Drain the fat off into a bowl.

3 To make the sauce, return the pan to the heat and deglaze with half of the stock. Add the rhubarb, cardamom, date syrup, cumin, cinnamon, and a bit of salt. Stir in the remaining stock and the water and bring to a simmer. Cover and cook for 10 minutes until the rhubarb has broken down fully, then remove the lid and reduce the sauce until it thickens a little, 5 to 10 minutes.

4 Serve the meatballs with the sauce and some steamed brown rice, the chopped pistachios, and cilantro leaves.

Serves 4

chicken breasts + red cacao sauce

Lean cuts like chicken breast call out to be paired with strong flavors. The superfood-packed Red Cacao Sauce does just that, adding spice, depth, and tomato richness to this simple meat. It is wonderful with the addition of the sesame brittle, for added crunch and a little subtle sweetness.

For the sesame brittle:
⅓ **cup sesame seeds**
1 tablespoon honey
Pinch of fine sea salt

For the chicken:
2 large boneless,
   skinless chicken breasts
Generous 2 cups chicken
   stock (page 8)
Big pinch of sea salt
Red Cacao Sauce
   (page 15), for serving
Cooked brown rice, for
   serving
Handful of cilantro
   leaves, for serving

Serves 2

1 To make the sesame brittle, preheat the oven to 350°F and line a baking sheet with greased parchment paper. In a bowl, mix the sesame seeds and honey together until the seeds are well coated then season with the salt. Transfer to the prepared baking sheet and spread out in a thin, even layer.

2 Bake for 10 to 12 minutes, until golden brown. Take care not to overcook. Let cool, then break into chunks.

3 To make the chicken, put the breasts in a pan and add enough stock to cover them. Add the salt, bring to a boil over medium-high heat, then decrease the heat to low, cover, and simmer gently for 8 to 10 minutes.

4 Remove the chicken from the cooking liquid and serve on a mound of brown rice. Spoon on some Red Cacao Sauce and top with sesame brittle and cilantro leaves.

seared steak, cashew + goji berry lettuce cups

These Asian steak cups can be served two ways, either as presented here, for appetizers or healthy finger food, or mixed together in a big salad bowl for a main course. My zesty Thai Dipping Sauce is the perfect complement.

14 ounces sirloin steaks
10 to 12 large leaves Boston lettuce
8 radishes, finely sliced
2 green onions, sliced
1 green chile, finely sliced
Small handful of mint and cilantro leaves
⅓ cup roasted cashews, coarsely chopped
Scant ½ cup goji berries
Thai Dipping Sauce (page 15), for serving

Serves 2 to 4

1 Heat a nonstick skillet over high heat, then sear the steaks for 2 to 3 minutes on each side, so they are very rare. Set aside to rest for 2 minutes, then cut into thin slices.

2 Meanwhile, arrange the lettuce leaves on a serving plate. Put the radishes, green onions, chile, herbs, cashews, goji berries, and beef into the lettuce cups. Serve with the dipping sauce alongside.

fennel + tarragon quinoa patties

As well as making wonderful patties, this mixture also makes delicious little quinoa balls. If cooking for a group, I often serve them as patties alongside a big bowl of leafy greens and a grain salad. But if it is just for a few people, I tend to make them smaller and serve in large lettuce cups with slivers of avocado, ripe cherry tomatoes, and lots of Cucumber, Radish + Goat Cheese Raita (see page 12).

Scant 1 cup quinoa
4 tablespoons coconut oil
1 onion, finely chopped
1 large fennel bulb,
  finely chopped
3 eggs, beaten
1 teaspoon fine sea salt
Scant ⅔ cup basil leaves,
  minced
¼ cup chives, minced
¼ cup tarragon leaves,
  minced
5¼ ounces crumbled
  soft goat cheese or feta
3 garlic cloves, minced
About 2 cups fresh
  rye or spelt bread
  crumbs

Serves 4

1 Rinse the quinoa well and put it in a small pan with enough cold water to cover by 1 inch. Bring to a boil, then decrease the heat, cover, and simmer for 15 to 20 minutes, until tender. Drain if necessary and set aside.

2 Meanwhile, heat 1 tablespoon of the coconut oil in a pan, add the onion and fennel, and cook over low heat, stirring occasionally, until soft and translucent, 10 to 15 minutes.

3 Make sure the cooked quinoa is thoroughly dry, then combine it with the eggs and salt in a bowl. Stir in the onion and fennel mixture and the basil, chives, tarragon, cheese, and garlic. Stir in enough bread crumbs to create a moist, sticky texture that holds together. Form the mixture into 12 patties.

4 Heat the remaining 3 tablespoons of coconut oil in a large, nonstick skillet over medium heat and cook the patties in batches (adding too many at once means they won't turn a nice golden color). Cook for 7 to 10 minutes on each side. If need be, increase the heat to form more of a golden crust. Transfer to a plate lined with paper towels while you cook the remaining patties.

butternut squash pearl barley pilaf

Pearl barley makes a delicious alternative to rice in this pilaf. The combination of the squash, dates, hazelnuts, and herbs adds contrasting sweetness, nuttiness, and crunch. It benefits from a squeeze of lemon and then all you need is a simple side salad to serve it with.

1½ pounds butternut squash flesh (about 1 small squash)
4 tablespoons extra-virgin olive oil
Sea salt and freshly ground black pepper
⅓ cup hazelnuts
2 garlic cloves, chopped
Scant 2 cups pearl barley
2 rosemary sprigs
4 cups hot chicken stock (page 8)
½ cup chopped pitted dates
4 green onions, finely sliced
Handful of flat-leaf parsley, chopped
Lemon wedges, for serving

Serves 4

1 Preheat the oven to 400°F. Cut the squash into small chunks. Spread out on a baking sheet, add 2 tablespoons of the oil, season generously with salt and pepper, and toss quickly to coat. Bake for 30 minutes, tossing the squash once halfway through, until it is tender and the edges are starting to caramelize.

2 Spread the hazelnuts out on another baking sheet and toast for about 10 minutes, until golden; you will be able to smell when they are done.

3 Heat the remaining 2 tablespoons of olive oil in a large saucepan. Add the garlic and fry for a couple of minutes, until it begins to turn golden. Add the barley and rosemary and stir to coat in the oil. Add the hot stock, bring to a boil, then decrease the heat and simmer for about 30 minutes, until the barley is tender and all the liquid has been absorbed.

4 Add the dates, green onions, roasted squash, and toasted hazelnuts and toss to combine. Cook over low heat for a few minutes to evaporate any excess moisture. Taste and season, then stir in half of the parsley.

5 Serve in bowls, topped with the remaining parsley and a squeeze of lemon.

smoked tofu panzanella with figs

Tofu is certainly a bit of a crowd divider. Often thought of as an ingredient used only by hardcore vegetarians or the more culinary brave, it tends to be underused. I am rather impartial to most varieties but a big fan of the smoked sort. I always buy organic, as nonorganic tofu is often made from genetically modified soybeans.

2 slices sourdough
  bread or thickly sliced
  gluten-free bread
Large handful of arugula
Small handful of basil
  leaves
Scant 3 cups cherry
  tomatoes, halved
7 ounces smoked tofu,
  cut into ¾-inch slices
2 large ripe figs, quartered
1 tablespoon extra-virgin
  olive oil
2 teaspoons apple cider
  vinegar
Sea salt and freshly ground
  black pepper
Basil Yogurt Dressing
  (page 14)

Serves 4 to 6

1 Heat a large grill pan over high heat until hot. Put the bread in the pan and place a lid on top to weigh it down. Toast until dark scorch marks appear, then flip it over and do the same on the other side. It should take 3 to 4 minutes on each side, but keep an eye on it.

2 Put the arugula and basil into a large bowl. Add the tomatoes, tofu, and figs, then drizzle with the olive oil and vinegar. Rip the charred bread into chunks and add to the bowl. Season with salt and pepper and toss gently to mix.

3 Serve with Basil Yogurt Dressing drizzled on top.

pure raw stripped bare **nude** clean detox

beet + orange quinoa granola

This nutty, crunchy granola is unlike conventional recipes. Not only is it packed full of mineral-dense beet, but it also has a much lower glycemic index due to the inclusion of quinoa, which is high in protein and low in carbohydrates, and a natural sweetener called stevia (see page 119). If you use maple syrup rather than stevia, omit the orange juice and use the maple syrup as the liquid to blend the beet. Enjoy with nut milk, yogurt, or sprinkled on top of smoothies.

Scant 2½ cups rolled oats
Scant ½ cup coarsely chopped hazelnuts
½ cup quinoa flakes
Scant 2 teaspoons ground cinnamon
¼ teaspoon sea salt
1 beet (3½ to 4½ ounces), peeled and coarsely chopped
Generous 2 tablespoons coconut oil
6 tablespoons date syrup, or 7 large pitted medjool dates soaked in ¼ cup hot water
⅔ cup maple syrup, or 20 drops vanilla stevia
2 teaspoons grated orange zest
2 to 3 tablespoons freshly squeezed orange juice, if needed
½ cup goji berries (optional)

Makes about 2 cups

1 Preheat the oven to 350°F.

2 Put the oats, hazelnuts, quinoa flakes, cinnamon, and salt into a large bowl. Briefly mix and set aside.

3 Put the beet, coconut oil, date syrup, maple syrup, and orange zest into a food processor. Process to make a sauce, adding orange juice if it seems too thick.

4 Pour the sauce over the oat mixture and stir well. Transfer to a greased baking sheet and use a spatula to smooth the mixture flat. Bake for 15 minutes, then remove from the oven and break into large pieces. Return to the oven and bake for another 10 minutes, then repeat the breaking-up process, stirring in the goji berries at this point, if using. Keep baking, turning the granola over every 10 minutes and breaking it up if necessary (you don't want it to be rubble) until crunchy and golden.

5 Store in an airtight glass container for up to 1 week.

toasted oatmeal with Earl Grey tea–soaked raisins

Cold days call out for warming nourishment. After too many breakfasts spent hopping around the kitchen scalding my mouth on a half-drunk cup of tea before rushing out the door, I tried a bit of an experiment and merged my morning cup with my breakfast. The result: a lovely balance of creamy and zesty, the only addition needed being a drizzle of maple syrup or honey to lift the sweetness of the raisins.

⅓ **cup plump raisins**

1 Earl Grey tea bag

½ **cup rolled oats**

½ **teaspoon finely grated orange zest, plus more for serving**

⅔ **to scant 1 cup almond milk, plus more for serving**

½ **teaspoon vanilla extract (optional)**

Sprinkling of unsweetened flaked dried coconut or almond slivers, for serving

Maple syrup, for serving

Serves 1

1 Put the raisins and tea bag in a mug and pour in just enough boiling water to cover. Let soak for 10 to 15 minutes, until infused.

2 Put the oats and orange zest in a pan over medium heat and toast, swirling the pan or stirring constantly, until they begin to release a lightly toasted aroma, about 5 minutes.

3 Remove the tea bag from the mug and set aside a few raisins for serving, then add the remaining raisins and soaking liquid to the oats, along with ⅔ cup of the almond milk and the vanilla, if using. As soon as the oatmeal starts to develop little bubbles, stir constantly and cook to the desired consistency, adding more milk if needed.

4 Transfer to a bowl and top with the reserved raisins, extra orange zest, and flaked coconut or slivered almonds. Serve with maple syrup and a little extra milk.

Tip
Use a chai tea bag instead of Earl Grey and add ½ teaspoon each of ground ginger and cinnamon— it's warming and nourishing for winter.

gluten-free chive crepes with avocado + smoked salmon

I often make up a full batch of these crepes and keep them in my refrigerator for quick and convenient wraps. The chives add flavor and color, but they are also delicious plain, and are the perfect vehicle for lots of fillings.

For the crepes:
Scant ⅔ **cup buckwheat or brown rice flour**
¼ **teaspoon fine sea salt (optional)**
1 **cup milk (any kind)**
3 **eggs**
Handful of chives, minced
Coconut oil, for cooking

For the salmon filling:
2 **large avocados**
9 **ounces hot- or cold-smoked salmon, flaked**
1 **lemon, cut into wedges**
Garlic Oil (page 10)
Freshly ground black pepper

Makes 6 to 8 crepes to serve 2 to 4

1 To make the crepes, mix the flour and salt, if using, in a large mixing bowl. In a separate bowl, whisk together the milk, eggs, and chives. Pour into the flour and stir until well combined and lump-free. Let sit for 5 minutes, then stir again and thin the mixture by adding water, a small splash at a time, until it has the consistency of heavy cream. (The right consistency is the key.)

2 To cook the crepes, heat a large nonstick skillet over medium heat. Melt a little coconut oil in the skillet, then pour in ¼ cup of the batter to thinly coat the bottom, rotating the pan as you pour so the batter spreads to cover the entire bottom. Cook until deep golden and the edges of the crepe are beginning to curl and lift. Flip and cook the second side.

3 Transfer to a plate, cover with a clean dish towel, and cook the remaining batter in the same way. Leftover batter keeps well in the refrigerator for a few days—just give it a stir and thin with a little water, if needed, before using.

4 To make the filling, halve, pit, peel, and thinly slice the avocados. Arrange some salmon and avocado in the center of each crepe, top with a squeeze of lemon, a drizzle of Garlic Oil, and a grinding of pepper. Roll up and eat.

coconut yogurt

This creamy, dairy-free yogurt alternative is a cultured food, packed with digestion-supporting probiotic enzymes. It is wonderfully smooth and creamy and works well as a base. I often add spices like cinnamon, ginger, and cardamom, or vanilla.

1 (14-ounce) can coconut milk, or 1 young green coconut and 3 to 6 tablespoons fermented probiotic kefir coconut water

1 capsule (or ½ teaspoon) any probiotic supplement to use as a starter

Natural fruit jam, for serving

Small handful of unsweetened flaked dried coconut, for serving

Makes 1¾ cups

1 Blend the coconut milk in a high-speed blender to achieve an even consistency. (If you are using the flesh of a young coconut to make the yogurt, add a little of the kefir coconut water to the blender along with the flesh. Start with 3 tablespoons of coconut water and add more gradually if needed. The amount you add will depend on the thickness you want to achieve.)

2 Once the coconut milk (or flesh and water) is smooth, add the probiotic supplement and stir well. The starter is what turns the coconut mixture into yogurt. Pour the mixture into a sterilized jar (see the ghee recipe on page 17) and keep at room temperature for 48 hours to let the cultures develop, and then store it in the refrigerator. It should keep for 3 to 4 days. To serve, top the yogurt with jam and flaked coconut.

orange blossom yogurt

Add ½ teaspoon orange blossom water and 2 teaspoons honey to the coconut yogurt in place of the jam and dried coconut.

Serves 2

almond + pine nut oat bars

Oat bars are one of my favorite afternoon treats. These contain nut butter rather than the usual oil or butter, which makes them much higher in protein. You can use homemade nut butter or a good-quality store-bought version. Cashew and pecan butters work particularly well.

3 cups rolled oats
¼ cup pine nuts
Scant ⅔ cup slivered almonds
½ cup chia seeds
Scant ⅔ cup dried cranberries
2 teaspoons ground cinnamon
2 teaspoons vanilla extract
⅔ cup maple syrup or honey
¾ cup unsalted nut butter
½ cup firmly packed coconut palm sugar
2 tablespoons water
Big pinch of sea salt

Makes 12 bars

1 Preheat the oven to 350°F. Grease a 12 by 8-inch baking pan and line with parchment paper.

2 Mix the oats, nuts, seeds, and cranberries in a bowl. Put the rest of the ingredients in a saucepan and stir over low heat until smooth. Add to the oat mixture and stir well.

3 Press the mixture into the pan and bake for 30 minutes, until golden. Let cool before cutting into bars. Store in an airtight container at room temperature for up to 4 days.

ultimate raw chocolate coins

These disks of chocolate heaven are best removed from the freezer and left to thaw for just 5 to 10 minutes before serving (any longer and they become too soft). Toasting the nuts is the real secret, as it gives a wonderful depth of flavor. If you are not familiar with it, stevia is a plant-based sugar alternative that lifts the sweetness of the cacao. You can buy it online in liquid form, or you can use ¼ cup coconut palm sugar in its place.

½ cup toasted pecans
½ cup raisins
½ cup pitted dates
½ cup toasted almonds
¼ cup raw cacao powder, plus
**   more for dusting, if needed**
1 tablespoon coconut oil
15 drops of vanilla stevia

Makes 12 to 14 coins

1 Process half of the pecans with the rest of the ingredients in a food processor until smooth. Chop the remaining pecans.

2 Transfer the mixture to a clean bowl and mix in the chopped pecans, then transfer to a sheet of plastic and roll into a sausage shape. If the mixture is very sticky, dust the surface with a little cacao powder.

3 Roll up in the plastic wrap, twist the ends to seal, and place in the freezer for 30 minutes to set. Cut into disks to serve. If you leave it in the freezer for any longer, remove it 5 to 10 minutes before slicing and serving.

flax + pumpkin gluten-free bread

I only recently developed this recipe and it has been a staple in my kitchen ever since. No one would ever know to look at it that it is completely grain-free and mostly carb-free, so it's perfect for anyone trying to cut back on their grain intake. It is undoubtedly at its best toasted, then dolloped, drizzled, or dressed with any toppings you fancy.

½ tablespoon coconut oil

1½ cups ground flaxseeds

Scant 2 cups ground almonds

1 tablespoon baking powder

1 teaspoon sea salt

½ cup pumpkin or sunflower seeds

Scant 1 cup water

5 eggs

Makes 1 small loaf

1 Preheat the oven to 350°F. Coat a small loaf pan (8½ by 4½ inches) with the coconut oil.

2 Put the flaxseeds, almonds, baking powder, salt, and three-quarters of the pumpkin seeds in a bowl and stir well. Add the water.

3 Beat the eggs in a large bowl until light and foamy, then combine with the flaxseed mixture. Gently stir to combine, keeping as much air in the eggs as you can, to make a thick but pourable batter. Pour into the prepared loaf pan.

4 Sprinkle the remaining pumpkin seeds over the top and bake for 35 to 40 minutes, until a toothpick inserted into the center of the bread comes out clean. Turn out onto a wire rack and let cool before slicing and serving. It will keep for up to 4 days in a sealed container at room temperature.

pure raw stripped bare rude **clean** detox

juicing

the popularity of juice

Let me ask you this: If you were to open your refrigerator on an average day, would you find a juice carton? I wouldn't be surprised if the answer is yes; juice is no longer considered a treat or a luxury item, but a refrigerator necessity, one of the staples that regularly makes its way into our shopping carts. The truth is that even those delicious crisp apple juices with no refined sugar and those punchy pomegranate juices supposedly packed full of antioxidants are often no better for us than sodas. True, juices vary in quality, but even those with the revered "no added sugar" are often pasteurized, damaging many vital nutrients.

juice diets

You may be familiar with the popularity of juice diets, usually a one- to three-day foodless fast, where the body is fueled by liquid alone. Despite the many declarations of their health-giving properties, I have found them to be impractical, exhausting, and thoroughly uninspiring. As you can imagine, surviving on liquid alone and very little fiber doesn't fill your body with vitality and energy. Granted, they have their benefits when it comes to weight loss and vitamins, but as with all diets, the results are short-lived. If the cleanse is not carried out properly, it is easy to miss out on a lot of the beneficial fats and proteins that the body needs to function effectively, leading to cravings and less healthy food choices once the cleanse is over. Juices are also often high in sugar, which, without the fruit and vegetable fiber, enters the bloodstream rapidly and results in peaks and lows of blood sugar levels. These are just a few of the reasons why I encourage any juice fanatic to approach juicing with responsibility and in conjunction with a healthy diet.

the benefits of fresh juice

It might sound at this point as if I am a bit of a juice skeptic, but au contraire: fresh juices are delicious and can be very beneficial, providing the body with a whole array of vitamins and minerals that are easily absorbed in the intestine because of their liquid form.

what is juicing?

Juicing is a process that separates the natural liquids from the fibrous structure of raw fruits and vegetables. It strips away any solid matter and leaves you with a liquid packed full of vitamins, minerals, antioxidants, anti-inflammatory compounds, and lots of phytonutrients, all ready and waiting in one convenient and hydrating drink.

types of juicers

centrifugal Most brands you see in stores are this type of juicer.
They spin at high speed, which separates the juice from the pulp.
In terms of price and efficiency, these are the obvious choice, but
the heat generated by the blade can destroy enzymes in the fruits
and vegetables.

cold-press/masticating The fruits and vegetables are crushed
and pressed hydraulically, which yields not only more juice, but also
more nutrients because the produce isn't heated up in order to extract
the juice.

what to juice

Of the many fruits and vegetables that can be juiced, these are my core
go-to naked ingredients. It is also possible to juice leafy greens (kale,
spinach, and chard), herbs, and berries, but whenever possible, blend
these ingredients to gain their full nutritional benefits.

fruits Lemon*, lime*, grapefruit*, orange*, kiwi*, apple, pear*, tomato,
pineapple*, melon*, watermelon*, grapes

vegetables Romaine lettuce, cucumber, fennel, broccoli stalk, carrot,
beet*, sweet potato, celery, parsnip

herbs + extras Ginger*, turmeric root*, chile, parsley, cilantro,
mint, basil

*Peel before juicing.

juices

supersalad juice

(pictured top right on opposite page)

This fruit-free juice is for the hard-core juicer. If it is too bitter for you, try swapping the celery for an apple.

2 celery stalks
½ cucumber
1 head romaine lettuce
Handful of spinach
1-inch piece of fresh
   peeled ginger

Makes about 2 cups

energy juice

Ginger and chile are both natural energizers, so this is a great juice to kick-start the system in the morning.

2 large beets
3 oranges, peel and pith
   removed
1-inch piece of fresh
   peeled ginger
¼ hot chile

Makes about 2 cups

happiness juice

(pictured middle right on opposite page)

This makes a wonderful smoothie if you blend it with a few ice cubes and the flesh of a ripe young coconut.

½ large pineapple, peeled and
   cored
2 apples
½ lemon, peel and pith removed
Handful of mint leaves

Makes about 2 cups

digestive juice

(pictured bottom left on opposite page)

Grapefruit works as a good cleanser, while the mint and fennel soothe and ease digestion.

1 cucumber
½ grapefruit, peel and pith
   removed
1 fennel bulb, including stalks
2 handfuls of spinach
2 to 4 mint sprigs
2 to 4 parsley sprigs

Makes about 2 cups

cleansing juice

1 fennel bulb, including stalks
2 large cucumbers, cut into
   shorter lengths
3 handfuls of baby spinach
Handful of parsley leaves
Handful of mint leaves

1 Put the fennel into the juicer and plunge. Put the pieces of one of the cucumbers in without plunging and fill the space around it with the baby spinach, then plunge. Do the same with the second cucumber, filling the gaps with the parsley and mint. This way the leafier greens get juiced well. Serve over ice.

Makes about 2 cups

homemade tomato juice

3 large tomatoes, sliced
2 celery stalks, halved
½ cucumber, peeled
½ lemon, peel and pith
   removed
¼ hot chile
Sea salt and freshly ground
   black pepper
A few drops of honey or
   maple syrup (optional)

1 Pass the tomatoes, celery, cucumber, lemon, and chile through the juicer. Season with salt and pepper to taste. Add the honey or maple syrup if you want it a little sweeter.

2 The juice has a tendency to separate, so strain it through dampened fine cheesecloth to remove any additional pulp if you wish.

Makes about 2 cups

naked lemonade

(pictured bottom right on opposite page)

A natural detoxicant and energizer, this is one of my favorite cleansing juices.

5 lemons, peel and pith
   removed
½ teaspoon cayenne pepper
1¾ cups coconut water
Scant 1 cup water

1 Juice the lemons, then stir together the juice, cayenne, and waters in a pitcher and serve.

Makes about 3 cups

smoothies

green goddess smoothie

(pictured top middle on page 97)

This thick, creamy smoothie is packed full of mineral-dense, anti-inflammatory ingredients. It is alwaysthe one I turn to if I am run-down, and is my go-toif I am suffering after a night of excess. It is perfect for keeping blood sugar levels balanced. If you are on a sugar-restricted diet, replace the banana with a couple of drops of liquid stevia.

3 large handfuls of leafy greens, such as spinach, chard, or kale
2 cups water
1 avocado
½ large banana
1 heaping tablespoon chopped fresh ginger
Juice of ½ lemon
2 tablespoons honey, or 2 to 3 pitted medjool dates
12 mint leaves (optional, for digestion)
3 to 4 drops of vanilla stevia (optional, for natural, sugar-free sweetness)
2 teaspoons spirulina, wheatgrass, chlorella, baobab, or lucuma powder (optional)
1 tablespoon tahini paste
Ice cubes (optional)
Bee pollen, for garnish

1 Put all of the ingredients except the bee pollen into a blender, adding ice if you'd like to chill the smoothie or thicken it. Garnish with bee pollen if desired.

Serves 2

spiced banana + pecan shake

(pictured top left on page 97)

This is a great postworkout smoothie because it contains the right mixture of protein, healthy fats, and potassium the body needs for recovery. The rich toasted nuts work wonders with the warm spices and sweet, toffee-tasting dates. The potassium-rich bananas are also high in amino acids, which trigger the body to produce the "happy" hormone serotonin. Use a nut milk of your choice.

½ cup pecans
2 cups unsweetened nut milk
1 large banana, peeled, chopped, and frozen
½ teaspoon ground cinnamon
½ teaspoon ground ginger
¼ teaspoon ground cloves
4 soft medjool dates, pitted
1 teaspoon lucuma powder (optional, for sweetness)
1 teaspoon maca powder (optional, for energy)
1 teaspoon baobab powder (optional, for vitamin C)

1 Preheat the oven to 350°F. Spread the pecans out on a baking sheet and roast for 15 minutes, until golden and toasted, then transfer to a blender.

2 Add half of the nut milk and blend until smooth. Add the remaining nut milk and the banana, spices, and dates, along with the lucuma powder, maca powder, and baobab powder as desired. Blend well.

Serves 2

beet + cherry smoothie

This dark purple, cacao-laced smoothie has a pleasing combination of earthy, rich, and zesty ingredients. It is filled with inflammation-fighting ginger and beet, to give your body vitamins and minerals it needs to reboot and refuel.

Scant ¼ cup hazelnuts or almonds or cashews
¾ cup frozen cherries
½-inch piece of fresh ginger
1 cup nut milk
1 beet, peeled and chopped
½ banana, frozen
1 teaspoon grated orange zest
1 heaping tablespoon raw cacao powder
2 tablespoons hemp protein (optional, for a
    post-exercise pick-me-up)
Small handful of oats (optional, for a more
    filling breakfast smoothie)

1 Preheat the oven to 350°F.

2 Spread the hazelnuts out on a baking sheet and roast in the oven for 15 minutes, then transfer to a blender. Add the remaining ingredients and blend until smooth.

Serves 2

berry + almond breakfast smoothie

(pictured middle right on opposite page)

This smoothie is best made with the almond butter, but anyone with a nut allergy can leave it out (instead, add 2 teaspoons coconut oil). It is a great source of many vitamins and minerals and a powerful anti-inflammatory that aids digestion. It also adds a smooth creaminess. If you fancy serving the smoothie in a bowl, with superfoods or granola sprinkled on top, decrease the amount of nut milk or add another tablespoon of oats to make it thick and spoonable (pictured bottom on opposite page).

1 banana
½ cup mixed blueberries and blackberries
1 to 2 tablespoons rolled oats
½ cup Naked Nut Milk (page 100) or Matcha
    Almond Milk (page 102)
1 heaping tablespoon almond butter
1 tablespoon chia seeds (optional, for omega-3s)
1 to 2 teaspoons honey (optional, for sweetness)
1 teaspoon lucuma powder (optional, for
    sweetness), maca powder (optional, for
    energy), or baobab powder (optional,
    for vitamin C)

1 Put all the ingredients in a blender and blend until smooth.

Tip
Using frozen berries and chunks of frozen banana will give you a thicker, frozen yogurt texture, which is also perfect as more of a soft-serve ice cream if you reduce the milk quantity.

Serves 1

nut milks

With so many grocery stores offering a variety of different nut milks, you may wonder whether it is worth making your own. The truth is that the majority of these store-bought products aren't as virtuous as they appear, and can contain stabilizers and emulsifiers, processed sugars, and a number of unnatural flavorings or sweeteners. They are also disappointing in flavor and texture.

If you have the time, it is certainly worth making nut milks from scratch and playing around with unique combinations that no store-bought product can offer.

soaking nuts

Nuts contain small amounts of phytic acid, a naturally occurring acid that prevents them from sprouting prematurely. Although this is not strictly harmful, it contains enzyme inhibitors and can be a strain on the digestive system. Soaking nuts before blending removes the phytic acid. Dissolve a pinch of salt in water and pour it over the nuts, using enough water to cover them. Leave in a warm place for the specified soaking time.

roasting nuts

Roasting or heating nuts before blending them into nut milk enhances their flavor, giving the finished milk a richness and depth not found when using raw nuts. I always roast them myself, as preroasted nuts tend to be higher in naturally occurring mold. They aren't unhealthy or necessarily harmful, but they aren't as nutritious as raw or soaked nuts.

sweeteners

Opt for natural sweeteners (see page 119) and stay away from high-fructose ingredients, such as agave. My preferred choices are maple syrup, date syrup, and liquid stevia. If you choose stevia, go easy on it, as 1 drop is equivalent to 1 heaping teaspoon of sugar.

types of blenders

High-speed blenders are certainly the best piece of kitchen equipment to invest in. They achieve a smooth, velvety texture for sauces, soups, nut milks, and smoothies.

However, they are not cheap, and they take up space in the kitchen, so it is worth looking at the options before you commit financially.

Vitamix: Undoubtedly the best for blending liquids, like soups, smoothies, and juices. The Vitamix is easy to use, with a manual knob to control the blending speed. However, it is large, so it takes up storage space.

Magimix: This is the type to use for larger-scale blending and making ground almonds and nut butter, grinding oats, etc. Every Magimix comes with three different bowl sizes. Like the Vitamix, it is a large piece of equipment, so it takes up storage space.

NutriBullet: Portable and convenient, with a sealable cup, it is the ideal blender to make single-portion smoothies and cold soups. It is not as powerful as the Vitamix, so it isn't ideal for blending more fibrous green smoothies. However, it is strong enough to grind small amounts of nuts or oats into flour and to make smaller amounts of nut butter.

supermilks

naked nut milk

*(pictured middle far right on
page 99)*

The simplest nut milk recipe. It is
a great dairy alternative to use in
place of regular milk, whenever
you fancy.

**1 cup nuts, soaked overnight
  in cold water**
4 cups water
1 tablespoon maple syrup
Pinch of sea salt

1 Drain the nuts and discard the
soaking water. Rinse the nuts,
then place them in a blender and
add the water, maple syrup, and
salt. Blend on high speed until
opaque and smooth.

2 If you want a smooth texture,
pour the milk into a strainer
lined with a large piece of damp
cheesecloth, set over a bowl or
pitcher, and let it run through into
the bowl. Gather the cheesecloth
around the nut mixture and twist
tightly closed. Squeeze and press
with your hands to extract as
much milk as possible. Do this for
at least 2 minutes.

3 Store in the refrigerator for
2 to 3 days.

**Makes 4 cups unstrained or
3½ cups strained**

hazelnut
chocolate milk

*(pictured bottom far right on
page 99)*

This healthy chocolate milk is
best used for nut shakes, iced
mochas, and hot chocolate.

**1⅔ cups hazelnuts, soaked for
  at least 2 hours in cold water**
3 cups water
**4 to 6 tablespoons raw cacao
  or cocoa powder, to taste**
**6 tablespoons maple syrup or
  honey, or to taste**
1 teaspoon ground cinnamon
Pinch of sea salt
2 teaspoons vanilla extract

1 Preheat the oven to 350°F.
Drain the hazelnuts, spread out
on a baking sheet, and roast in
the oven for 15 minutes, then
transfer to a blender.

2 Add the water and process
for 2 minutes, until the liquid
has turned white and the nuts
are no longer visible.

3 Transfer the mixture to a
strainer lined with a large piece
of damp cheesecloth, set over a
bowl or a pitcher. Let the milk run
through the strainer into the bowl
or pitcher beneath, then gather
the cheesecloth around the nut
mixture and twist tightly closed.
Squeeze and press with your
hands to extract as much milk
as possible. Do this for at least
2 minutes.

4 Rinse out the blender and pour
in the filtered milk. Add the cacao
powder, maple syrup, cinnamon,
salt, and vanilla extract. Blend
again to combine. Store in the
refrigerator for 2 to 3 days.

Makes 4 cups

avocado milk

(pictured middle left on page 99)

This nut milk is great for both savory and sweet recipes. Blend it into smoothies, or use it instead of milk in pancakes with some spinach and feta for a savory option. Serve cold, add to smoothies, or pour over cereal.

Scant ½ cup blanched almonds, soaked for at least 2 hours in cold water
4 cups water
½ avocado
3 to 4 tablespoons maple syrup
2 teaspoons vanilla extract
Pinch of sea salt

1 Drain the almonds, discarding the soaking water, rinse them, and put into a blender with the water. Process for 2 minutes, until the liquid has turned white and the nuts are no longer visible.

2 Transfer the mixture to a strainer lined with a large piece of damp cheesecloth, set over a bowl or a pitcher. Let the milk run through the strainer into the bowl or pitcher beneath, then gather the cheesecloth around the nut mixture and twist tightly closed. Squeeze and press with your hands to extract as much milk as possible. Do this for at least 2 minutes.

3 Rinse out the blender and pour in the filtered milk. Add the avocado, maple syrup to taste, vanilla, and salt and process until smooth, adding a little extra water to thin, if you like.

4 Store in the refrigerator for up to 2 days.

Makes about 4 cups

macadamia + maca milk

(pictured top left on page 99)

The creaminess of macadamia nuts complements the earthy taste of maca powder (the Peruvian superfood) really well. Pour over granola for a omega-superfood boost.

1⅔ cups macadamias, soaked for 2 hours in cold water
4 cups water
4 teaspoons maca powder
1 teaspoon vanilla extract
Maple syrup or other sweetener, to taste

1 Drain the macadamias, discarding the soaking water, rinse them, and put into a blender with the water. Blend for 2 minutes, until the liquid has turned white and the nuts are no longer visible.

2 Transfer the mixture to a strainer lined with a large piece of damp cheesecloth, set over a bowl or pitcher. Let the milk run through the strainer into the bowl beneath, then gather the cheesecloth around the nut mixture and twist tightly closed. Squeeze and press with your hands to extract as much milk as possible. Do this for at least 2 minutes.

3 Rinse out the blender and pour in the filtered milk. Add the maca powder, vanilla, and maple syrup, then blend to combine. Store in the refrigerator for up to 3 days.

Makes about 4 cups

sesame seed milk

The longer you soak the seeds, the better: 24 to 48 hours is ideal, as it activates the seeds, making them more digestible. They also blend to a creamier, smoother texture.

1⅓ cups sesame seeds, soaked 24 to 48 hours in cold water
4 cups water
Small pinch of sea salt
4 drops of vanilla stevia, or 2 tablespoons maple syrup and 1 teaspoon vanilla extract

1 Drain the sesame seeds, discarding the soaking water. Put into a blender with half of the water, the salt, and the stevia and process until fully combined and smooth. Add the remaining water and blend briefly.

2 If you want a smooth texture, pour the milk into a strainer lined with a large piece of damp cheesecloth, set over a bowl or pitcher, and let it run through into the bowl. Gather the cheesecloth around the seed mixture and twist tightly closed. Squeeze and press with your hands to extract as much milk as possible. Do this for at least 2 minutes.

3 Store in the refrigerator for up to 4 days.

Makes 4 cups unstrained or 3½ cups strained

vanilla caramel milk

Serve this cold, or heat it in a saucepan for a creamy hot chocolate alternative, or to add to tea or coffee.

1¾ cups cashews, soaked
 for at least 2 hours in
 cold water
12 soft medjool dates, pitted
 and chopped
4 cups water
2 to 4 tablespoons maple syrup
 and 2 teaspoons vanilla
 extract, or 4 to 6 drops vanilla
 stevia
Pinch of sea salt

1 Drain the cashews, discarding the soaking water, rinse well, then put into a blender with the dates and 3⅓ cups of the water. Blend for 2 minutes, until the liquid has turned white and the cashews are no longer visible, adding more water if needed.

2 Transfer the mixture to a strainer lined with a large piece of damp cheesecloth, set over a bowl. Let the milk run through the strainer into the bowl beneath, then gather the cloth around the nut mixture and twist tightly closed. Squeeze and press with your hands to extract as much milk as possible. Do this for at least 2 minutes.

3 Rinse out the blender and pour in the filtered milk. Add the maple syrup and vanilla to taste and the salt and blend again to combine. Store in the refrigerator for 2 to 3 days.

Makes about 4 cups

matcha almond milk

(pictured bottom middle on page 99)

This is a beverage rather than a base nut milk. It's a refreshing, summery alternative to caffe latte and is best served cold, poured over ice.

1⅔ cups blanched almonds,
 soaked for at least 2 hours
 in cold water
4 cups water
2 tablespoons matcha green
 tea powder
1 teaspoon vanilla extract
Maple syrup or sweetener
 of choice, to taste

1 Drain the almonds, discarding the soaking water, rinse well, and put into a blender with the water. Blend for 2 minutes, until the liquid has turned white and the nuts are no longer visible.

2 Transfer the mixture to a strainer lined with a large piece of damp cheesecloth, set over a bowl. Let the milk run through the strainer into the bowl beneath, then gather the cloth around the nut mixture and twist tightly closed. Squeeze and press with your hands to extract as much milk as possible. Do this for at least 2 minutes.

3 Rinse out the blender and pour in the filtered milk. Add the matcha powder, vanilla, and maple syrup to taste, then blend to combine. Store in the refrigerator for up to 4 days.

Makes about 4 cups

pistachio + wheatgrass milk

Blending in a quarter of an avocado (similar to the Avocado Milk on page 101) when you add the sweetener makes this milk taste amazing and adds a creamy texture.

1⅔ cups pistachios, soaked for
 at least 4 hours in cold water
4 cups water
4 teaspoons wheatgrass
 powder
Maple syrup or sweetener
 of choice, to taste

1 Drain the pistachios, discarding the soaking water, rinse well, and put into a blender with the water. Blend for 2 minutes, until the liquid has turned white and the nuts are no longer visible.

2 Transfer the mixture to a strainer lined with a large piece of damp cheesecloth, set over a bowl. Let the milk run through the strainer into the bowl beneath, then gather the cloth around the nut mixture and twist tightly closed. Squeeze and press with your hands to extract as much milk as possible. Do this for at least 2 minutes.

3 Rinse out the blender and pour in the filtered milk. Add the wheatgrass powder and maple syrup and blend again to combine. Store in the refrigerator for 2 to 3 days.

Makes about 4 cups

lattes

Frothing milk takes a bit of skill. However, it can be made simpler by opting for a thicker milk. As with all lattes, an electric milk frother is the secret weapon! Also, when heating the milk, it's best to begin frothing it when it reaches room temperature to ensure that you get good volume.

chai latte

(pictured middle right on page 104)

I associate chai with my time spent in India, where it is made and drunk all across the country. I would often frequent the tiny tea stalls on roadsides or buy a 5-rupee cup from a chai wallah on train journeys. The spices in the tea makes it delicious, and they also have a lot of medicinal benefits. This spice mix quantity is a lot more than you need for this recipe, but it's worth making as it stores well in a dry place in an airtight jar, out of direct sunlight. The milk you use is completely up you. I opt for oat or almond milk.

For the chai masala mix:
    cup cardamom seeds
¾ cup black peppercorns
½ cup ground ginger
3 tablespoons ground cinnamon
1   teaspoon ground cloves
1   teaspoon ground nutmeg

1 cup milk (any kind), plus more for serving
1 to 2 teaspoons honey or maple syrup
1 chai tea bag

1 To make the chai masala mix, grind the cardamom seeds and peppercorns together using a mortar and pestle, then mix all the spices together.

2 In a small saucepan, combine the milk, honey, tea bag, and ⅛ to ¼ teaspoon chai masala mix, according to taste. Place over medium heat and, before it comes to a boil, remove from the heat and stir well. Let steep for 5 minutes, then remove the tea bag and heat again, until hot but not boiling. Garnish with a drizzle of milk.

Serves 1

coffee + cacao latte

(pictured top right on page 104)

The difference between cocoa and cacao is simply in the processing: cacao is unrefined and unroasted, and therefore much higher in beneficial minerals and vitamins, whereas cocoa has been roasted at a high temperature, lowering its nutritional value and making it more bitter. Although I recommend cacao, you can also use cocoa here, reducing it to 1½ tablespoons because of its extra bitterness. The milk you use is completely up you. I opt for oat or almond milk.

2 tablespoons raw cacao powder, plus a pinch
    for serving
Scant 1 cup milk (any kind)
2 drops of vanilla stevia, or 2 teaspoons
    maple syrup
1 shot espresso or scant ¼ cup strong
    coffee

1 Put the cacao powder and half of the milk in a pan over medium-low heat. As it heats up, whisk the mixture using an electric milk frother to get rid of any lumps. Once smooth, add the remaining milk and the vanilla stevia and continue frothing.

2 Pour the espresso into a mug, then pour in the cacao milk, holding back the foam with a spoon. Spoon the foam over the top and add a pinch of cacao before slurping.

Serves 1

turmeric + ginger latte

(pictured top left on opposite page)

This warming beverage is one of my favorite cold-busting drinks. Referring to it as a latte is a tad misleading, as it is actually caffeine-free (which makes it a great evening tipple). To increase its medicinal benefits, feel free to swap the ground ginger for 1 teaspoon of freshly extracted ginger juice. The milk you use is completely up you. I opt for oat or almond milk.

1 teaspoon ground turmeric
½ teaspoon ground cinnamon
⅛ teaspoon ground ginger
1 cup milk (any kind)
½ teaspoon honey, or to taste

1 Lightly toast the spices in a dry skillet for a couple of minutes, stirring occasionally, until they start to smell fragrant.

2 Slowly add the milk, watching out for splattering. Froth using an electric milk frother until bubbles form, then sweeten to taste with the honey. Pour into a cup and enjoy.

Serves 1

matcha + vanilla latte

(pictured bottom left on opposite page)

Matcha is a powdered green tea from Japan, made from high-grade, antioxidant-rich leaves. It makes for a wonderful latte alternative, giving a slow release of energy and providing the body with a number of beneficial vitamins and minerals. The milk you use is completely up you. I opt for oat or almond milk.

1 teaspoon matcha green tea powder
1 cup milk (any kind)
1 drop of vanilla stevia, or ½ teaspoon maple syrup, or to taste

1 Put the matcha powder in a cup and gradually add a scant ¼ cup of the milk, frothing using an electric milk frother, until dissolved. Warm the remaining milk in a saucepan, whisking as it heats up and becomes light and aerated, then add the dissolved matcha. Continue frothing until hot, then sweeten to taste with the stevia. Enjoy hot, or cold over ice.

Serves 1

ices

energizing lemon + honey granita

(pictured left on opposite page)

This light, refreshing treat is a real favorite and acts as a great palate cleanser between courses at dinner parties. Use the best quality tea bags you can find, as it makes a great difference to the flavor.

4 green tea bags
2-inch piece of fresh ginger, grated
3 cups boiling water
2/3 cup honey
6 tablespoons freshly squeezed lemon juice

1 Put the tea bags and ginger in a bowl and pour in the boiling water. Cover and let stand for 15 minutes. Remove the tea bags and let cool slightly.

2 Add the honey and lemon juice and stir to combine. Strain through a strainer into a bowl and cool completely, then pour the mixture into an 8-inch square baking dish or something similar. Cover and freeze for 8 hours or until firm.

3 Remove from the freezer and scrape with a fork until fluffy. Serve.

Makes about 4 cups

mango + coconut ice cream

(pictured right on opposite page)

Sometimes a sorbet doesn't quite do the job. This is an alternative ice cream recipe that I came up with for one of my cooking students, who is allergic to eggs; it's creamy and rich and melts beautifully.

2 large ripe mangoes
Finely grated zest and juice of 1 lemon
1-inch piece of fresh ginger, grated
Generous 1 cup honey or maple syrup
Generous 2 cups canned coconut milk

1 Peel the mangoes and cut the flesh into pieces. Add to a saucepan with the lemon zest and ginger. If the mangoes aren't really ripe, add a few tablespoons of water.

2 Cook over medium heat, stirring often, for 10 minutes, until tender. Decrease the heat and simmer for 15 to 20 minutes, stirring occasionally, until the mangoes have a jamlike consistency.

3 Remove from the heat and cool to room temperature. Transfer to a food processor, add the rest of the ingredients, and process briefly; don't overmix, as it's nice with some fruit pieces. Chill in the refrigerator before churning in an ice cream machine for about 25 minutes, or according to the machine's directions. If not serving right away, store it in the freezer.

Makes about 4 cups

prune + bitter chocolate frozen ricotta

(pictured left on opposite page)

Rich, creamy, and wickedly chocolaty, this recipe is packed full of fiber from the prunes and antioxidants from the raw cacao. It is even better if you use homemade ricotta, too (see page 12). This is a decadent after-dinner dessert with a shot of coffee.

Generous 1 cup ricotta
Generous 1 cup plain Greek yogurt
1 cup pitted and chopped prunes
Generous ¼ cup raw cacao powder
6 tablespoons coconut palm sugar
1 cup walnuts (optional)
Scant ½ cup brandy or rum (optional)
Pinch of sea salt
Generous ¾ cup raw cacao nibs, for serving

1 Put all the ingredients except the cacao nibs into a blender and blend until fully smooth.

2 Churn in an ice-cream machine for 45 minutes. Transfer to a container and freeze for a couple of hours.

3 Serve sprinkled with the cacao nibs.

Makes 4 cups

plum + amaretto sorbet

(pictured right on opposite page)

I make this recipe in big batches in the late summer months when my mother's plum tree starts dropping its ripe wares in abundance. It's a favorite because it's so refreshingly light and sugar-free, yet has a hefty kick from the amaretto.

2 pounds plums, pitted and sliced into eighths
1¼ cups maple syrup
1 vanilla bean
2 tablespoons amaretto

1 Preheat the oven to 400°F.

2 Put the plum pieces in a bowl, add the maple syrup, and toss to mix. Let stand for 5 minutes, then transfer to a roasting pan, reserving the liquid left behind in the bowl. Slit the vanilla bean lengthwise, chop into a few pieces, and add to the pan.

3 Roast for about 30 minutes, until the plums are really soft and slightly blistered around the edges. Transfer to a strainer set over a bowl and press the mixture through. Add the amaretto and reserved maple syrup liquid to the strained mixture.

4 Churn the mixture in an ice-cream maker according to the machine's directions. Transfer to a container and freeze for 3 to 4 hours, until set. In the absence of an ice cream maker, pour the mixture into a sealable container and place it in the freezer. Remove the container from the freezer every 20 minutes and stir the sorbet; repeat this step until the sorbet is completely frozen and smooth.

Makes 4 cups

cocktails

smoky bloody Mary

(pictured top left and bottom right on opposite page)

This hybrid is the classic bloody Mary with a smoky twist. I have a real affinity for this lively version, which slips down rather too easily. If you are using homemade tomato juice, be sure to add a good grinding of black pepper, too.

4 cups Homemade Tomato Juice (page 92), chilled
1 tablespoon tomato paste
2 to 3 teaspoons Tabasco, or to taste
1 teaspoon Worcestershire sauce
1½ teaspoons sweet smoked paprika
1 teaspoon celery salt
1 lime, cut into wedges
Freshly ground black pepper
1¼ cups vodka (ideally smoked vodka)
Celery stalks, for serving (optional)

1 In a large pitcher, mix together the tomato juice, tomato paste, Tabasco, Worcestershire sauce, paprika, and celery salt. Squeeze each lime wedge into the pitcher, leaving some juice in each. Stir well.

2 Grind in some pepper, then taste and adjust the level of heat as desired. Drop the lime wedges into the pitcher and stir well. Cover and chill for at least 30 minutes.

3 Pour the vodka into the pitcher and stir well. Serve immediately, with a grinding of pepper and a stalk of celery.

Serves 4

lychee + mint margaritas

(pictured top right and bottom left on opposite page)

Refreshing, light, and clean tasting, this is the perfect blended summer cocktail. If you fancy, you can serve them on the rocks with the addition of coconut water—it's a great way to rebalance the body and keep you hydrated.

6 fresh lychees, pitted and chopped, plus 2 fresh lychees, pitted and halved, for serving
1 cup ice cubes
1 cup freshly squeezed lime juice
Generous ⅓ cup triple sec or Cointreau
Generous ⅓ cup tequila
Lime wedges, for serving
Coarse sea salt, for serving
4 mint sprigs, for serving

1 Put the lychees, ice, lime juice, triple sec, and tequila in a blender and process until smooth.

2 Use the lime wedges to moisten the rims of 4 glasses, then dip the rims into coarse sea salt to coat. Pour the mixture into glasses and garnish each with a mint sprig, lime wedge, and lychee half.

Tip
To serve on the rocks, omit the ice from the blended ingredients and distribute the ice cubes among 4 glasses. Divide the blended mixture between the glasses and top off with coconut water. Garnish as directed.

Serves 4

detox

why detox

Every day we are exposed to harmful toxins and chemicals, which enter the body through the air we breathe, the food we eat, and the water we drink. Detoxing is about ridding the body of these built-up toxins, helping it to regenerate cells and improve overall health and vitality. True, you might say, our bodies already have a built-in system to flush these toxins out, but at times our sophisticated internal systems get overwhelmed and stop functioning at their fullest capacity.

Detoxing is all about optimizing that system. It involves eating whole foods packed with nutrients in order to boost the activity of the body's enzymes and nourish your most important detoxifying organs—the liver, lungs, kidneys, and colon—so ultimately they can do their jobs better and more efficiently.

when to detox

The time to detox is often the time you want to do it the least, such as when you are running on low, feeling flat and unmotivated. At times like this, it is easy to turn toward caffeine, energy drinks, and sugar to keep you going, but there's a more effective solution—good old-fashioned detoxification. You may find it hard to believe that short-term dietary adjustments can be the answer to give you back lost energy, but short detoxes can help jump-start weight loss, eliminate cravings, wake up the digestive system, and introduce you to a new way of eating: a mindful eating practice.

how to detox

A major component of any detox or cleanse is a healthy diet. Why? Detoxification programs that combine short-term dietary changes with nourishing foods that support the liver's detoxification enzyme systems have been shown to significantly reduce tiredness, pain, and other symptoms in patients with chronic fatigue syndrome, fibromyalgia, and other chronic conditions. The dietary component of a detox cleanse typically involves making short-term dietary adjustments that are designed to accomplish a number of objectives.

You can detox easily and effectively while you continue to eat, as long as you are cutting out the foods and substances that interfere with the detoxification process. Processed foods should be avoided— nothing from a box, jar, or can. You want to eat only fresh food (organic, if possible) starting with three days and, if strong, going up to ten.

digestion detox

what is the digestion detox?

The digestive system is the gateway to the body, the interface and protective barrier between you and the outside world. It acts like a skin on the inside, keeping out the bad stuff and letting the good stuff in, taking in food, breaking it down, and turning it into a liquid form from which we can absorb its nutrients.

We have an amazing digestive system that allows for a range of different types of foods to be processed, and the body's ability to do this is crucial to our overall health. An impaired system can be detrimental to not only our energy but also our mood, immunity, and quality of life. In the most simple terms, we should all be aware of just how effectively our bodies process and absorb the nutrients from the food and drinks we consume, because there is nothing more important than having a fully functioning digestive system.

The quality and nutritional properties of the food we eat play a vital role in maintaining the balance of bacteria in the digestive tract. Having a balanced gut flora is crucial to its ability to process foods. The increase in prepackaged, convenience, and highly processed foods can largely be blamed for the increase in the number of people suffering digestive issues and diseases. Digestive imbalances can manifest themselves in many forms, from the severe cases of Crohn's disease, colitis, and leaky gut to undiagnosed irritable bowel syndrome (IBS), chronic fatigue, and candida overgrowth. Although not all of these conditions can be cured by diet alone, eating well-balanced, nutritionally dense foods helps to heal and support digestion in its daily functioning. As a long-term sufferer of postinfectious IBS, I have firsthand experience of the improvements the body feels when it is given the correct foods it needs for optimal functioning.

the mouth

The mouth accomplishes the first step in the digestive process. Chewing food thoroughly breaks down the larger pieces of food into smaller particles, making it easier for the stomach to break down. It is also where food is first exposed to amylase, an enzyme created by the salivary glands, which assists in breaking down food, contributing to the overall chemical process of digestion.

small mouthfuls

There is a 20-minute window while eating before the brain signals to the stomach that we are full. Eating slowly, with smaller mouthfuls, gives the body time to determine whether it is full and can prevent accidental overeating.

chewing food

I don't advocate any specific number of times you should chew food, as ultimately you should take an approach that works best for you. When chewing your food, try not to think of the number of times you have chewed it, but instead the enjoyment of eating it. Chewing your food completely until it is small enough to be swallowed with ease will help you get a sense of your own eating patterns and help you develop a relationship with the food you consume. The saliva produced when chewing also relaxes the lower stomach (pylorus) muscles, aiding the food's progress through your stomach and into your small intestine.

the stomach

The next stage of the digestive process takes place in the stomach, where a hormone called gastrin (which relates to acid secretion) is produced in response to the presence of food. The acid in the stomach is responsible for killing off bacteria and other microorganisms that enter the body with food. It also breaks down proteins, activates digestive enzymes, and facilitates later absorption in the intestine. Part of successfully processing the food in the stomach requires having a balanced level of acidity.

stomach acidity test

First thing in the morning, before eating or drinking anything, mix ¼ teaspoon of baking soda into a scant 1 cup of cold water. Drink the solution and time how long it takes for you to start burping. If your stomach is producing adequate amounts of hydrochloric acid, you will burp after 2 to 3 minutes. Early or repeated belching is due to an excessive amount of stomach acid.

high acidity

Often, excessively high or low stomach acidity may display very similar symptoms, such as heartburn, gastric ulcers, and acid reflux, so it is important to correctly identify which problem is occurring in order to prevent inappropriate treatment. Try to identify foods that contribute to excess stomach acid and aid the healing by eating natural anti-inflammatory foods, such as ginger, turmeric, and mineral-rich greens and vegetables. Eliminate salty, spicy, highly processed (premade) food, sugar, alcohol, and caffeinated foods and beverages. Remember, if your body is off balance, it takes time for it to return to its equilibrium, so be patient and allow it the time it needs.

low acidity

When the stomach's pH is high (and its acid level low), food takes longer to digest, which can result in fermentation and issues with bacterial overgrowth. There are many natural ways to increase the natural production of stomach acid. Try mixing 1 tablespoon of raw apple cider vinegar with 2 tablespoons of warm water and drinking it first thing in the morning, 15 minutes before eating. Another method is drinking a large glass of water before meals. Contrary to popular belief, drinking water before meals actually triggers the production of stomach acid. The water prepares the body for food, prompting the intestine to produce mucus to protect the intestine from the stomach acid, thus allowing the stomach to make more acid and process the food properly.

sensitive stomach

When the stomach feels weak, it is advisable to eat foods that are easily digestible. Avoiding excessive consumption of raw fruits and vegetables during times of more sensitive digestion is advisable, as the plant cell walls are made of cellulose fibers that the digestive system struggles to break down. When uncooked, these cell walls are harder for the body to break down, requiring more energy. Warm, nourishing soups and rice-based dishes like the Yoga Bowl (page 26) and drinks like Turmeric + Ginger Latte (page 105) are soothing options.

cleansing foods for the stomach

sea salt Although salt should be used in careful moderation, a little can have beneficial effects. High-mineral sea salt stimulates acid production in the stomach.
lemon Drinking hot water with fresh lemon throughout the day is cleansing for the stomach, as it acts as a natural detoxicant and decongestant. It is beneficial to drink first thing in the morning, before eating, to prepare the stomach for food.
ginger A natural digestive that can be used to treat various types of stomach ailments. Try making an infusion with lemon juice and hot water, juicing it, or blending it into smoothies.

healing foods for the stomach

miso soup Made from fermented soybeans, it acts as a natural probiotic due to the microorganisms used in the fermentation process. It also contains high amounts of easily absorbable zinc (good for immunity) and manganese (assists the thyroid and regulates metabolic rate).
oats A neutral, plain-tasting food, oats are best eaten in the form of oatmeal to soothe the stomach. They are also high in beneficial vitamins and minerals and a good source of fiber.

brown rice Washed thoroughly and cooked properly, rice makes a good stomach soother because it is neutral and therefore doesn't irritate the stomach. It is also a good source of fiber.

the intestine

Made up of the large and the small intestine, this organ is one of the largest and most complex in the body. The intestinal tract relies on the presence of beneficial bacteria to support its specialized immune-supporting cells and a complex network of neurological and hormonal components. It acts as the headquarters for immunity and neurological health, housing the tools for breaking down food and also numerous nerve endings and sensors that relate directly to our immune, hormonal, and nervous systems. The gut is also home to the largest concentration of mood-altering neurotransmitters, with around 80 percent of our serotonin receptors.

a note on IBS

Having tried many different diets, the one I have found most useful in easing symptoms of IBS is the low-FODMAP diet. It advocates the restriction of all highly fermentible short-chain carbohydrates, which are often poorly digested in the small intestine, causing rapid fermentation in the gut, exacerbating the symptoms of IBS. The research is relatively new and being developed all the time. If IBS is something you suffer with, it is certainly a diet to look into (under the guidance of a registered dietitian).

cleansing foods + spices for the intestine

grapefruit Grapefruit is rich in the insoluble fiber pectin, which, by acting as a bulk laxative, helps to protect the colon mucous membrane by decreasing exposure time to toxic substances in the colon. It also facilitates dietary iron absorption from the intestine. Eat whole or as juice, or use the juice for smoothies.

turmeric The yellow or orange pigment of turmeric, curcumin, has long been used as a treatment for inflammatory bowel disease (IBD), such as Crohn's and ulcerative colitis. It is a beneficial ingredient that can be used in a number of dishes, from curries to dressings, and is also delicious as a tea.

oily fish They reduce inflammation and help in healing the digestive tract lining. They can also improve nutrient absorption, help balance hormones, improve neurological function, and boost immunity.

healing foods + herbs for the intestine

peppermint The ultimate herb to stimulate the flow of digestive juices and ease cramps. Add it to salads, salsas, and Asian dishes, or infuse the leaves in hot water for a soothing, digestive tea.

fennel An effective digestive and antispasmodic, fennel decreases bloating, heartburn, and gas. It can be eaten both raw in salads and cooked.

cultured fermented foods Fermented foods are known to support the balance of beneficial bacteria in the gut. These include foods like kimchi and sauerkraut, both made of fermented cabbage (pages 32 and 33) and also miso, made from fermented soybeans.

energy detox

what is the energy detox?

The entire focus of this cleanse is geared toward improving the body's energy generation system. Most diets cause tiredness, loss of energy, and lack of motivation. Usually this is due to an insufficient amount of calories. When we are detoxing and cleansing the system, the body needs fuel to work properly.

We often need look no further than the quality of food in our daily meals to see the association between food and fatigue. Just think about the heavy distended feeling you have after eating a large meal. Food should fill us with vitality and energy, not make us want to pass out. The energy cleanse focuses on the foods that do just that, by removing the things we rely on for social energy (namely alcohol, sugar, and caffeine), emphasizing key foods that stimulate the organs (liver and kidneys) responsible for rebooting our energy stores, and encouraging toxin elimination.

why do the detox?

When we are feeling low and energy depleted, it is too easy to rely on borrowed energy, in the form of caffeine, sugar, nicotine, or alcohol. In the short run they keep the body ticking, but in the long run they impair the adrenals, kidney, and liver, and we find ourselves in a spiral of continual fatigue. Stimulant foods and drinks are also acid forming and break down the body's resistance and immunity.

When enjoyed in moderation and as part of a balanced diet, these substances are not necessarily a negative thing. In fact, they can be quite positive. Coffee is known to improve cognitive function and increase the amount of dopamine released by the brain. Red wine is known to be high in resveratrol, a beneficial, heart-healthy antioxidant found in very few foods. It is only once the body becomes reliant upon them that they become a problem. Stimulation requires restimulation to alleviate the downswing of the initial indulgence.

Having experienced the effects of caffeine and sugar dependence firsthand, I fully understand how all-consuming they can be and how giving them up, or even cutting back on them, can seem impossible. In truth, sometimes it gets a little bit harder before it gets easier. This is why giving them up, cold turkey, for five days is key. It's just a chance to give the body a well-deserved break and to help restore the body with healing foods and drinks that rebalance the organs most responsible for keeping you energized and awake.

a note about salt

An excess of sodium encourages our cells to store water, giving the body a heavy, sluggish feeling. During this time of detox, cut your salt intake significantly; you will certainly notice the difference. In place of added salt, you can use herbs and spices to enhance the flavors in dishes.

liver

One of the largest organs in the body, the liver mainly acts as a filter for the blood coming from the digestive tract, passing it to the rest of the body. It also performs many essential functions related to digestion, metabolism, immunity, and the storage of nutrients within the body. This includes storing glycogen (fuel for the body), processing fats and proteins from digested food, processing medicines and chemicals, and removing poisons and toxins taken in by the body.

what it is affected by

Enzymes in the liver are responsible for metabolizing alcohol, sugar, and drugs. A poor diet, unhealthy weight, lack of exercise, and high cholesterol are all factors that directly affect its capacity to function.

cut out the chemicals

Any harmful chemicals, pesticides, and other food sprays that your intestine cannot digest are passed through to the liver to process. Not only are they harmful for the function of the liver in the short term, but over longer periods of time they can build up in the body, causing disease and longer-term health issues. Although our exposure to chemicals cannot be removed completely, here are a few ways of reducing your intake:
• Choose organic or higher-welfare meat, dairy, and eggs whenever possible. Buy the best you can afford.
• Wash all fruits and vegetables thoroughly before using, especially if they are nonorganic.
• Buy a water filter; even just a water bottle with a filter is useful to help purify your water when you are on the go.
• Switch your cleaning sprays and soaps to natural products.
• Limit excessive consumption of high-fructose foods, as the body cannot assimilate fructose and an excess of it leads to fat buildup in the liver.

cleansing foods + spices for the liver

broccoli It contains a phytochemical called sulforaphane, which naturally stimulates the liver's detoxifying.
green tea A plant full of antioxidants known as catechins, known to assist liver function.
turmeric A powerful anti-inflammatory used to treat a wide variety of conditions.

healing foods + spices for the liver

avocado It stimulates the production of glutathione, an essential nutrient for liver health.
cinnamon This helps support the liver by reducing the triglyceride response after eating.

kidneys

The role of the kidneys is to balance pH levels and salt in the blood, to keep blood composition constant. It is their job to remove excess water and waste liquids, which get secreted from the kidneys as urine. If your kidneys are not functioning properly, accumulated waste can build up in both the kidneys and the blood.

what they are affected by

High blood pressure can damage blood vessels in the kidneys, reducing their ability to work properly. If these blood vessels get damaged, they become less able to remove waste and fluids from the body, which in turn can increase blood pressure levels further. Unlike the stomach and intestines, the kidneys never sees food, so they are only affected on a secondary level.

go veggie for a day Instead of eating meat daily, try going vegetarian for two days a week. A vegetable- and fruit-based diet allows the body system to alkalinize via the kidneys.

cleansing foods, spices + herbs for the kidney

parsley An important diuretic, parsley helps clear uric acid from the urinary tract and helps dissolve and expel gallstones.
dandelion leaves + roots These have been used for centuries to treat liver, gall bladder, kidney, and joint problems. They are also a natural source of potassium and will replenish any that may be lost due to the diuretic action of other kidney-cleansing herbs, such as parsley and marshmallow root.
marshmallow root It has a directly soothing effect on inflamed and irritated tissues of the alimentary canal and urinary and respiratory organs. It also has components that eliminate toxins, helping the body to cleanse.

healing foods, spices + herbs for the kidney

chamomile Acts as an anti-inflammatory and eases pain, infection, and allergy, most commonly cystitis.

cranberry Commonly used to help prevent and treat urinary tract infections, it also helps to kill germs and speed skin healing.

nettles These have natural anti-inflammatory properties and also improve urine flow and the expulsion of water from the body, helping to flush bacteria out of the urinary tract.

adrenals

The adrenal glands manage adrenaline production and regulate blood sugar levels. They are also affected when a person is under stress, and if a person is in a constant state of physical or emotional stress, the adrenals become fatigued and stop functioning optimally. This is known as adrenal fatigue or exhaustion.

what they are affected by

Caffeine and sugar both have a big effect on the adrenal glands, stimulating them and giving the body a short-term booster of mental and physical energy, which makes us feel more capable and motivated. This injection of energy is an overexertion that the body has to make up for afterward. When our adrenal glands are constantly required to sustain high adrenaline levels, they eventually become impaired in their ability to respond appropriately. It is adrenaline that is responsible for the little burst of energy that wakes us up in the morning, and for keeping us awake, alert, and focused throughout the rest of the day. Needless to say, these glands are crucial to our health. Symptoms of adrenal fatigue include tiredness that is not relieved by sleep, salt cravings, difficulty focusing, poor memory, and inability to cope with stress. The adrenals are also affected by emotional stress.

supplements + herbs to rebalance the adrenals

vitamin C A critical vitamin for stress reduction and adrenal health, vitamin C is used by the adrenal glands in the production of all of the adrenal hormones, most notably cortisol. In adrenal fatigue, your adrenal glands release more cortisol when faced with a vitamin C deficiency. This increases immediate anxiety and prolongs a state of high cortisol, which is bad for blood sugar and blood pressure and contributes to the storing of fat in the body.

magnesium Magnesium plays a role in the function of more than three hundred enzymes in the human body. If you are magnesium-deficient, the point at which your adrenals kick in to produce fight-or-flight hormones is lower. Eating food high in magnesium can help improve this.

ashwagandha + ginseng Both of these are good adaptogens, which help the adrenals adjust to stress. Both are also potent antioxidants, help improve immune function, and work to decrease anxiety.

licorice It supports the production of cortisol and has long been used to support adrenal health. It supports the immune system and helps ease fatigue, pain, and weakness associated with adrenal depletion.

detox note

If you feel you are suffering from any of the symptoms outlined in this text, do seek out the help of a registered doctor, dietitian, or nutritionist for a full diagnosis.

the naked pantry

Although I tend to let fresh produce dictate the base of most of
my meals, I always keep my pantry stocked with natural "naked"
essentials—ingredients I can reach for to produce the recipes I love
to eat and cook on a daily basis. Having a well-stocked pantry means
always being prepared, and gives any cook flexibility and a reliable
ingredient source to work from.

Throughout the years, my pantry has seen many ingredients
come and go. Freekeh, bulgur, barberries, you name it. I am always
interested in trying every new and unpronounceable grain, flour,
noodle, or spice that crosses my path.

Despite my excitement for new finds, if you were to look into my
pantry on any given day, you would always find a selection of key,
foundation items—the naked backbone of my cooking. Most of the
ingredients I use are readily available in most larger grocery stores,
but unfortunately many local smaller spots don't tend to stock kamut
flour or farro grains. I can't for the life of me think why not . . . it would
serve the world a whole lot better if they swapped the bright, magpie-
luring confectionery for hearty whole grains. Anyway, it just takes a little
preparation, a bit of online shopping, or a trip to a slightly larger grocery
store every now and then.

In the process of writing this book, I did a lot of research with family
and friends, asking them where they felt they would like to improve their
diet and what their main obstacles were in acheiving it. One of the most
recurring answers for the latter was habit and routine. Having a well-
stocked pantry makes it that much easier to choose healthier options
when it comes to daily dishes. Even the cook with the best of intentions
can be lured by quick-cooking, refined ingredients when their whole
grain counterparts are not available.

In an attempt to move away from the processed, refined, and
abundant quantity of bleached white foods that fill many pantries, here
is a list of alternatives. These are the staple, unprocessed, unrefined
"naked" ingredients that are the foundations of *The Naked Cookbook*.

flours

The more familiar varieties of flour are made from cereal grains (such as wheat, spelt, and rye), but flours are also made from ground beans, nuts, fruits, and seeds. One thing to consider when choosing a flour is what you are intending to use it for, as the way one flour functions is different than another, and it's not as simple as substituting one kind for another.

almond Usually made from ground blanched almonds, this is a favorite for grain-free and low-carb baking. It is high in omega-3 fats. I like to buy whole, unblanched almonds and grind my own in a high-speed blender, which I store in a sealed jar.

brown rice + buckwheat Both of these are gluten-free and often used in baking. They can be used alone but work best when combined with other flours. Although from different sources, they yield similar results in cooking and are interchangeable.

coconut A good gluten-free, low-carb, nut-free flour alternative, coconut flour contains more dietary fiber than other wheat alternatives and is naturally high in beneficial fats.

cornstarch This is the powdered starch of the corn grain, and although it lacks the beneficial husk and germ of the corn, its fineness makes it a very useful, gluten-free thickening agent.

gluten-free Gluten-free flour can be made from many foods that don't contain gluten. Mostly these are not grains, but beans, seeds, or nuts. Most of the gluten-free flour you see on the shelves of grocery stores is the processed white variety, which has a high glycemic index (GI), is low in nutrition, and contains little fiber. I tend to use brown rice or buckwheat flour.

kamut Also known as Khorasan flour, kamut is an ancient variety of wheat, originally grown for the pharaohs in Egypt. It is naturally high in protein and minerals such as selenium. It has a higher level of gluten than spelt and is good for homemade pasta and bread.

polenta This is a grainy meal made from coarsely ground corn. It is best to buy stone-ground, as the hull and germ are still attached, giving it more flavor and a higher nutritional value.

rye Naturally lower in gluten than wheat, rye has a rich, deep flavor. It is best to buy stone-ground whole rye flour. Although rye contains gluten, it tends to give heavy results, so when baking use it mixed with other flours, which lightens the flavor and gives a better rise.

spelt An ancient variety of wheat, with a lower GI and a higher profile of nutrients, spelt contains gluten, but in lower quantities than traditional wheat. It is easier to digest than most grains and is recommended as a wheat alternative for people with poor digestion and irritable gut. The flour can be bought either white or whole grain, has a nutty taste, and can be used for making breads and other baking.

sweeteners

Natural sweeteners have a lower GI than processed refined sugar and contain more beneficial nutrients. As with flour, I generally steer clear of anything white, and keep a range of different types in the pantry for varying flavors. There are a lot of sugars and sweeteners to be wary of. High-fructose sugars, like agave nectar or "fruit-based" sweeteners, are often marketed as a healthy sugar alternative, when actually they are highly processed, poorly digested, and strain the liver.

blackstrap molasses Molasses is the dark, syrupy by-product from the process of sugar extraction from sugarcane. It is important to buy organic and unsulfured, which contains all the minerals and nutrients of the sugarcane.

coconut palm sugar Also called jaggery, this is available in granulated form, has a much lower GI than regular cane sugar, and is a great alternative for healthy baking. It's rich and treacly in flavor, like soft brown sugar.

date syrup A sweetener made from dates, its flavor is like a marriage of blackstrap molasses and maple syrup. Not too sweet, it has a rich, deep flavor.

honey A natural source of sugar, honey is known for its healing properties, especially manuka honey from New Zealand and Australia. Always buy raw honey, as it hasn't been heated or processed in any way and will have all the enzymes intact. I recommend avoiding heating honey to over 104°F, because this will change its molecular structure.

maple syrup Made from the sap of maple trees, this naturally occurring sugar has a lower GI than honey.

stevia This natural sweetener has no calories and no impact on GI and is therefore suitable for diabetics. It is available in a range of different flavors. I like vanilla, and often substitute stevia for half of another variety of sugar. It is best in liquid form. One drop is as sweet as 1 teaspoon of coconut palm sugar.

grains + beans

Not only are grains and beans cheap and delicious, they also contain a lot of beneficial nutrients that are overlooked when we condemn their ground, milled, overused counterparts. I like to have at least one day a week without eating meat and find grain-based dishes the most satisfying and filling. As they are in their whole form, they have a much lower GI and are higher in fiber. Eaten in combination with fresh, seasonal vegetables, roasted nuts, and fresh herbs, these grains and beans form the foundation of some of my favorite dishes.

brown basmati A variety of long-grain rice from the Indian subcontinent, brown basmati still contains its bran. It is high in fiber and beneficial vitamins and can be used in place of white rice.

farro + spelt Farro is a whole grain often used in Italian cooking that looks similar to pearl barley but has a nuttier flavor. It retains its shape when cooked, so it works well in salads. Spelt is also known as dinkel wheat or hulled wheat. Both are useful ingredients and are pretty interchangeable between dishes. be used in place of white rice.

pearl barley Not to be confused with whole grain barley, this is the barley grain with the bran and hull removed. It takes on a creamy texture when cooked and can be used in place of rice in risottos.

quinoa This South American seed is often noted for its high protein and low carbohydrate levels. It is a good gluten-free

alternative to grain and has a range of different colors. I favor the dramatic black and red varieties for their appearance, although the cooking time and taste of all colors is very similar.

red rice Often from the Camargue region of France, this short-grained rice has a slightly nutty taste and chewy texture.

cannellini + lima beans High in protein and low in fat, both varieties of white bean are very mild in flavor and thus a versatile staple. Dried are best but require soaking.

chickpeas One of the most versatile beans, chickpeas are a useful staple to have on hand for quick salads, stews, soups, or dips. They are high in protein and low in fat, making them a good meat substitute. Buying dried is best, but cooking requires soaking, so if time is an issue, opt for the canned variety, preferably organic.

Le puy lentils These lentils hold their shape when cooked, making them good for salads. It is best to soak them before use; not only does this reduce the cooking time, it also reduces a natural, nondigestible phytic acid that often can lead to digestive discomfort.

red lentils There are many lentil varieties, with red being best for making dals, curries, and stews, as they are lower in fiber than the Le puy variety. About 30 percent of their calories are from protein, making them the third highest protein source of any bean or nut. They also have a high iron content.

fruits, nuts + seeds

dates Best bought dried, dates are sweet, high in fiber and a

number of vitamins and minerals, and useful for bringing sweetness to savory dishes, as well as to smoothies and desserts.

dried cherries + currants These are tarter and tend to be a little smaller than raisins. They are very versatile. I use them in savory dishes, such as rice salads.

goji berries High in antioxidants and minerals, these dried berries have been used in Chinese medicine for years. They are less sweet than raisins, but without the tartness of sour cherries. I add them to granola, smoothies, and salads, for color and texture.

golden raisins + raisins Both can be used in anything from baking to smoothies. Soaking them in liquid before using plumps them up.

unsweetened shredded + flaked dried coconut Made from the flesh of the coconut, these are gluten-free and have a low GI. Shredded takes the form of small flecks, with flaked tending to be slightly larger. Both are great additions to baking or can be simply sprinkled over yogurt or oatmeal at breakfast time.

almonds One of the most popular and versatile of nuts, almonds make a great pantry staple. They are best bought whole, raw, and with skins on. You can roast them or blend them into milk or flour. They are also good to have on hand for a healthy snack.

cashews One of the milder flavored nuts, cashews have a high oil content, which means they blend very well into a thick, creamy texture. They are ideal for making nut butter. As they are high in mold, anyone suffering from issues with

interchangeable, but a mixed selection is always best.

sesame seeds Small and intense in flavor, these make a great addition to Asian dishes. I often have a pot of them toasted by my stove to add a sprinkle to finish off dishes. They also work well for making a mild-flavored nut milk.

spices + herbs

Spices are a wonderful way to pack complex flavors into simple dishes. They often have a lot of health benefits in their own right and have been used for years in traditional medicine to treat ailments and support good health, especially in the digestive tract. It is best to buy spices whole and grind them yourself, in small batches, as they lose their potency after a few months. Herbs are very much a subjective choice, depending on the foods and cuisines you tend to gravitate toward in your cooking.

bay leaves Whenever I find a bay tree, I pick a large handful of leaves and put them in a warm place to dry out. They are useful for adding depth of flavor and richness to meat, soups, and stews, as well as to sweet dishes. Try infusing a couple of leaves in milk, especially when making hot chocolate.

cardamom This aromatic spice, which comes in different varieties, is most recognizable as small seeds encased in a green pod. It is best bought in whole pods and ground down, to retain freshness. Cardamom can ease indigestion and excess stomach acid.

cayenne pepper Found in ground form, from a South American variety of hot red chile, cayenne adds heat and spice to dishes. It also helps

candida in the gut is advised to avoid eating cashews.

hazelnuts One of my two favorite nuts, hazelnuts are undoubtedly at their best when toasted. I buy them in the fall (often in their shell) and crack them myself. They find their way into anything from salads to granola, nut milks, and smoothies.

pecans My other favorite nut, pecans are sweet, rich, and complex in flavor and can be easily bought whole, halved, or chopped. Undoubtedly at their best when toasted, they work wonders with sweet-tasting ingredients, especially chocolate, maple syrup, and sweet potatoes.

pistachios Often used in Middle Eastern cooking, pistachios add a delicious flavor and a lovely pop of color to so many sweet and savory dishes. They are also

a member of the cashew family and, as such, can have a high mold content and not advisable for people with candida.

pine nuts Slightly more expensive than other nuts, with a high oil content and a unique flavor, pine nuts make a classic addition to salads but also work superbly well in sweet dishes. I like to pair them with dried cranberries in my nut butter bars.

chia seeds Small and black, these look like poppy seeds and are one of the highest vegetarian sources of omega-3 fats. When soaked, they break down and become gelatinous, making them ideal for baking and smoothies, but not ideal for sprinkling on salads.

mixed seeds The variety of seeds I have varies. Sometimes it is a jar of flaxseed, sunflower, and pumpkin. Generally they are

the body to flush out toxins and stimulates weight loss by boosting metabolism.

cinnamon With its naturally sweet taste, cinnamon is one of the most popular spices in baking. It can be bought in stick form or ground. It stays fresh longer when bought whole, but ground is certainly more convenient. Cinnamon is known to aid digestion and helps to fight bacterial infections.

coriander seeds These dried berries of the cilantro herb have a deeper, different taste than the fresh stems and leaves. For best results, buy them whole and grind them yourself.

cumin seeds The seeds of a small plant in the parsley family, these have a distinctive earthy flavor and are commonly used in Middle Eastern and Indian cooking. For best results, buy them whole and grind them yourself.

kaffir lime leaves A popular ingredient in southeast Asian cooking, these are best bought and used fresh, but having them dried is handy for times when they are hard to come by. They add a distinctive, floral freshness and vibrancy to soups, curries, and seasoning pastes.

nutmeg Whole nutmegs come as small egg-shaped seeds and have a rich, slightly sweet taste. For best results, buy them whole and grate them. Nutmeg contains the compounds myristicin and elemicin, both known to stimulate mental activity.

red pepper flakes These are a dried and crushed version of red chiles with seeds, most commonly made from ancho or cayenne chiles. They add heat and flavor, but also color, to dishes. Chiles

are also known to improve blood circulation and boost energy levels.

rosemary Useful for flavoring, rosemary is a popular herb in many dishes. Try drying branches of rosemary yourself by tying string to the end and hanging it in a warm place to dry out. Break off the leaves and store in a sealed container for handy use.

saffron The most expensive spice, obtained from the stamen of a crocus, saffron is mild in flavor, so other spices should be used lightly so as not to mask it. It also gives food a wonderful yellow color.

smoked paprika Made from the *Capsicum annuum* chile, smoked paprika can be smooth, sweet, or spicy depending on the variety. I buy both a Spanish spicy variety and the sweet sort as well. It adds a wonderful richness and depth to dishes and dressings.

thyme A popular herb for flavoring dishes, thyme can be dried in the same way as rosemary.

oils + condiments

Oils can be extracted from a number of different sources. The best ones to use are those with minimal processing, which more often than not means cold-pressed, extra-virgin, and organic oils. These oils have been produced in a way that retains the highest amount of nutritional components possible and are beneficial for good health.

There are three categories of fat: saturated, monounsaturated, and polyunsaturated. Saturated fats are made up of saturated triglycerides (fat) only and are most commonly found in dairy products and fatty meats. They tend to harden to a solid at room

temperature. Coconut oil and ghee are both saturated fats, and although saturated fats are often condemned as bad, this is not strictly the case, as both of these have many health benefits and remain stable at higher cooking temperatures. Monounsaturated fats are fats that remain liquid at room temperature. They have a thicker viscosity than polyunsaturates, which makes them more suited to use in cooking. Polyunsaturates, on the other hand, have a very thin viscosity at all temperatures. They also have a delicate molecular structure, so are not ideal to cook with and are better used to finish dishes or in dressings.

extra-virgin olive oil My favorite of all oils, this is the highest quality and most expensive olive oil. It is suitable for cooking, but only at low temperatures. I love the distinctive grassy notes and often use it as a condiment or in dressings. It is best to buy fresh pressed and organic.

ghee This is clarified butter, made by extracting the oil from butter and discarding the milk solids. It is about two-thirds a saturated fat, which means it remains stable at higher temperatures. This makes it ideal for panfrying and sautéing, giving dishes that wonderful, rich buttery flavor without the risk of burning the milk solids in butter.

infused oils Infusing oils is quick and easy to do and I always have a bottle of garlic oil on the go. I tend to do this with a lesser quality, but still organic, olive oil, as it has a milder flavor and takes on the taste of the infusing ingredient better. It is suitable for cooking, but at low temperatures only.

toasted sesame oil This rich, strong-flavored oil is extracted from toasted sesame seeds. It is not a stable oil to cook with and therefore better as a condiment or dressing. As it is very distinctive in flavor, it is best used sparingly.

virgin coconut oil Coconut oil is extracted from the kernel or meat of matured coconuts. It is great for cooking with as, unlike other oils, it remains stable at high temperatures. However, because it is a saturated fat it sets hard at room temperature and also has a mild, sweet coconut flavor that isn't ideal for dressings. It has a whole host of health benefits, including boosting metabolism, and is a source of the powerful antiviral and antibacterial lauric acid.

balsamic vinegar The king of all vinegars. I am never without a bottle of good-quality balsamic. Like olive oil, you get what you pay for, and it is worth investing in a higher-quality variety. It adds richness and sweetness as well as a vinegary kick to dishes.

raw apple cider vinegar It is best to buy raw and unfiltered cider vinegar as it has the beneficial living enzymes in the vinegar. This variety is alkaline-forming in the body and known for its nutrients and health benefits.

chyawanprash This jamlike cooked mixture of honey, ghee, triphala, and many other herbs and spices is used in Ayurvedic medicine as a supplement. It can also be added to hot drinks, such as hot water with honey and lemon juice.

Dijon mustard The traditional creamy, pale yellow French mustard.

fish sauce An amber-colored liquid extracted from the fermentation of anchovies with sea salt, it is used in Asian cooking.

nut butter This form of spreadable nuts can be bought or made, and used in a vast number of dishes. All types offer different benefits in terms of taste and health. The most versatile are certainly almond, cashew, and peanut butter, and these tend to be the ones I buy.

orange blossom water Distilled from orange blossoms, this has a very distinctive and refreshing citrus-floral flavor. It is quite strong and should be used sparingly.

rose water Made from a distillate of rose petals, rose water is a by-product of rose oil production for perfume. Particularly popular in Middle Eastern food, it adds a floral taste and can be used in both savory and sweet dishes.

tahini A rich paste made from ground, hulled sesame seeds, tahini is essentially sesame seed butter. I use it widely, including in dips, dressings, and even smoothies.

tamari Tamari is a form of soy sauce, traditionally made as a by-product of miso production. It tastes a lot like soy sauce but is often gluten-free.

cereals

There are vast numbers of different grains, flakes, and cereals on the market. For the sake of storage space and necessity I try to keep my pantry condensed into a few key essentials. Most health food stores will stock them, and if not, they can be found online.

buckwheat groats These are raw, unprocessed buckwheat kernels that can be roasted or sprouted. They are naturally gluten-free and make a great addition to granola and muesli.

oats A staple cereal grain that I use practically daily in savory and sweet dishes, oats are a slow-release carbohydrate, filled with fiber. They can be bought gluten-free too.

quinoa flakes Made from unprocessed, flattened quinoa seeds, these are high in protein and beneficial omega-3 fatty acids, and are also lower in carbohydrates than most grains. They can be used for anything from breakfast to baking and are naturally gluten-free.

spelt flakes I often use these as a substitute for oats in dishes when I am looking for a richer flavor. As the spelt grain is related to wheat, it does contain a small amount of gluten, but is easily digestible.

superfoods

A lot of hype surrounds superfoods and their benefits. Although there is no guarantee that eating superfoods will drastically change your health, they are all rich in vitamins and minerals and, as such, can make a beneficial addition to the diet.

ashwagandha Made from Indian winter cherry, this is one of the most beneficial herbs in Ayurvedic medicine, known for its restorative benefits and immune system support. It has an earthy, bonfire, bitter taste.

baobab Originating from the tree of the same name in Africa, baobab is 50 percent fiber and is extremely high in vitamin C and beneficial B vitamins. It has a distinct, citrusy taste and is best used stirred into oatmeal and sprinkled on cereal.

bee pollen This is the pollen packed by worker honeybees into small granules with added nectar, and is very high in amino acids. It has a pleasing sweet taste and works as a good natural sweetener for smoothies and raw desserts.

chlorella A variety of blue-green algae available in powder form, chlorella contains the highest levels of chlorophyll found in any edible plant. Its taste is even less appetizing than spirulina, so it may be best taken in tablet form, rather then used as a powdered ingredient.

lucuma A naturally sweet subtropical fruit native to the Andean valleys of Peru, lucuma makes a delicious addition to shakes, smoothies, and desserts. It is also nice simply stirred into yogurt and served with fresh berries.

maca This root is also called Peruvian ginseng and has an earthy, deep caramel flavor. Most commonly available in powder form, it is known to improve energy and boost vitality and libido in both men and women.

mesquite This superfood, extracted from the pods of the mesquite tree, is high in fiber and calcium. It has a rich, spiced flavor, a little like a combination of coffee, cacao, and cinnamon, and is best for sweet dishes and smoothies.

raw cacao Raw cacao is made by cold pressing unroasted cocoa beans, a process that preserves the living enzymes in the cocoa. Raw cacao is also high in resveratrol, an antioxidant that helps protect the nervous system. It can be bought as nibs or ground.

reishi mushrooms They are a herbal mushroom used in Chinese medicine and one of the oldest to be used medicinally. They are high in antioxidants, good for boosting the immune system, and thought to fight the growth of cancerous cells. They are bitter in taste, so best consumed dried as a powder or as tablets.

shatavari Derived from a variety of asparagus, this beneficial herb is commonly used in Ayurvedic medicine to support the female reproductive system. It can help with mood swings and PMS, as well as menopausal hot flashes. It can be bought as a powder and has a sweet and bitter taste.

spirulina This type of blue-green algae, most commonly bought in powder form, is largely made up of protein and essential amino acids. It can be added to juices and smoothies, but sparingly, as it is not the most pleasant-tasting of superfoods.

wheatgrass Wheatgrass, the leaves of young wheat plants, is often used fresh but can be bought in powder form. It is a much sweeter-tasting green superfood than chlorella or spirulina and gives dishes and smoothies a vibrant green color.

index

Acknowledgments

To my parents who have supported me, Fred who loved me, and Humphrey who cured me. Also all the wonderful support from the brilliant minds of all my wonderful friends, editors, agents, students, and teachers. Thank you for keeping me inspired.

This is a book for all the budding cooks, food lovers, and aspiring healthy eaters. It is a way to live, love, and eat today and every day—with real, unprocessed, and "naked" foods.

I hope it makes you as happy to read and cook from as it made me to write and taste.

With love
Tess

Text copyright © 2015 by Tess Ward
Photographs copyright © 2015 by
Columbus Leth
Design and layout © 2015
Quadrille Publishing

All rights reserved.
Published in the United States by Ten Speed
Press, an imprint of the Crown Publishing
Group, a division of Penguin Random House
LLC, New York.
www.crownpublishing.com
www.tenspeed.com

Ten Speed Press and the Ten Speed Press
colophon are registered trademarks of
Penguin Random House LLC.

Originally published in hardcover in Great
Britain as *The Naked Diet* by Quadrille
Publishing Ltd., London, in 2015.

Library of Congress Cataloging-in-
Publication Data

Names: Ward, Tess, 1990- author. I
Leth, Columbus, photographer.
Title: The naked cookbook / Tess Ward ;
photography by Columbus Leth.
Description: First American edition. I
Berkeley : Ten Speed Press, [2016]

Includes index.
Identifiers: LCCN 2015039084
Subjects: LCSH: Cooking (Natural foods) I
Health. I LCGFT: Cookbooks.
Classification: LCC TX741 .W3683 2016 I
DDC 641.3/02–dc23 LC record
available at http://lccn.loc.gov/2015039084.

Hardcover ISBN: 978-1-60774-994-3
eBook ISBN: 978-1-60774-995-0
Printed in China

Design by Quadrille Publishing

Publishing director: Sarah Lavelle
Creative director: Helen Lewis
Editor: Romilly Morgan
Copy editor: Sally Somers
Design: Katherine Keeble
Photography: Columbus Leth
Food stylist: Rukmini Iyer
Props stylist: Rachel Jukes
Production: Vincent Smith,
Stephen Lang

10 9 8 7 6 5 4 3 2 1

First American Edition